410   S551881

RESOURCES IN SCHOOLS

Library Association Guidelines for School Libraries

Edited by Margaret Kinnell

LIBRARY ASSOCIATION PUBLISHING
LONDON

Published by
Library Association Publishing Ltd
7 Ridgmount Street
London WC1E 7AE

First published 1992

British Library Cataloguing in Publication Data

Learning Resources in Schools: Library Association Guidelines for School Libraries
   I. Kinnell, Margaret
   027.8

   ISBN 1-85604-032-1

Typeset in 10/12pt Palacio by Library Association Publishing Ltd
Printed and made in Great Britain by Amber (Printwork) Ltd, Harpenden, Herts

CONTENTS

Preface

Ross Shimmon

School libraries are, or should be, an integral part of the educational process. Indeed a government report published in 1984 argued that they are the 'foundations of the curriculum'. Yet, in the United Kingdom the provision of school libraries has for the most part fallen short of the ideal and, compared with standards in libraries in higher education, is often scandalously poor.

The Library Association has long campaigned for greater recognition of the essential role of school libraries. It has argued for better training of teachers in the use of libraries and the teaching of information skills, the appointment of professional librarians in schools, and the provision of an appropriate number and quality of books and other learning materials in well located, furnished and equipped libraries.

In the United Kingdom it has been the practice in most education authorities to supplement individual school libraries by Schools Library Services often administered by the public library service. These long-awaited guidelines contain The Library Association's views and recommendations on the necessary level of provision of both the individual school library and the centrally provided Schools Library Service. They have been prepared by The Association's Working Party on Learning Resources in Schools chaired by Wendy Drewett. They were approved as official Library Association guidelines by The Library and Information Services Committee of Library Association Council in 1991. They have been edited by Margaret Kinnell.

FOREWORD

A S Robertson

Good libraries empower. Using their resources can unfetter our imaginations; disclose hitherto unrealized worlds; promote knowledge; induce pleasure; make us laugh; impart insights; challenge our preconceptions; assuage fears; prick our conscience; inflame our sensibilities; and provide professional refreshment. What we learn from good books and other resources becomes part of us.

Children and young people are entitled to the best – a range and depth of learning resources appropriate to their personal, social, emotional and intellectual needs. Each generation benefits from the guidance and instruction of expert librarians and sensitive teachers. Before pupils become independent users of information they need to learn which resources to choose, how to find and select information and how to make the best use of it. They also need to be helped to make effective use of a wider range of resources and information available through the newer technologies. Never has the necessity been greater for young people to develop sufficient confidence to discriminate wisely – between the average, the mediocre and the best – and to demand and use the best.

Good libraries don't happen by chance. The best are developed rationally – frequently by a whole-school community, often with the energetic support of a school library service. The proper provision and cost-effective use of learning resources is cardinal to promoting enhanced classroom achievement and high educational standards. For a school not to invest time and energy in promoting its learning resources is to disadvantage its pupils.

These guidelines are based on the best practice which is already a reality in some schools. Not all young people are habitual library users, however; not all pupils are sufficiently well versed in learning strategies. These guidelines will assist schools, librarians, teachers and school library services, whatever their present circumstances, to plan library advance. The recommendations, when implemented, will help secure our children's richer future.

GLOSSARY OF TERMS

Chartered librarian
A chartered librarian is a graduate who has either completed a three-year undergraduate or a one-year postgraduate course in Library and Information Studies (which is recognized by The Library Association as offering the appropriate professional education), and in addition has fulfilled the training and professional requirements of The Library Association.

School library and information services
These are the sum of the resources, facilities and services provided by the school library resource centre to meet the learning resources needs of the school.

School library resource centre
The school library resource centre provides a centrally located base from which the library and information service is delivered to the school. There may be more than one library resource centre in a multi-site school.

Schools Library Service
This is the service which is provided, usually either by the public library service as an agent of the Local Education Authority or direct by the Education Authority itself, to support the work of library and information services in schools.

SUMMARY

These Guidelines have been prepared at a time of great change in the learning resources needs of schools. The most fundamental changes are contained in the provisions of the 1988 Education Reform Act which introduced the National Curriculum and Local Management of Schools for England and Wales; similar changes are occurring in the rest of the UK.

Management and staffing structures
An effective and efficient system for the provision, organization, management and utilization of all the learning resources in a school is essential. This is best achieved through the provision of a centralized school library resource centre, with the services of professional, chartered librarians who are trained in the provision, organization, management and utilization of resources and information.

Provision of accommodation
The increasingly important role of the school library resource centre has been recognized in the large number of new and adapted library spaces that have been created in schools in recent years. The function and use, siting, amount of space required, allocation of space, furniture and equipment, and administrative accommodation of school library resource centres all have to be considered in designing library and information services for schools. Schools Library Service advisory staff have a particularly important role to play in this planning activity.

Learning resources: management and organization
The acquisition and management of learning resources, which needs to be a feature of the School Plan, should ensure that all school library resource centre collections include a rich variety of media available in supporting the curriculum. The curriculum

demands that students have direct access to larger quantities of a widening range of resources. A selection policy is particularly important, as it provides the validity for the resources base; and the quantitative guidelines offered here are a useful template against which the needs of individual schools may be matched.

Learning skills

The use of learning resources needs to be planned within a whole-school learning skills policy; learning skills, like all other skills, need to be learned and practised. Every school needs a regular curriculum audit to identify those learning skills that are required at every stage in a child's school career. The Head of Library and Information Services within the school should play a key role in this cross-curricular audit.

Schools Library Service

The process of school library resource centre development, and the use of learning resources in the curriculum, have been guided and supported by Schools Library Services. The knowledge and experience of chartered librarians in such services have provided elected members and officers with advice and direction. As schools meet the challenge of Local Management of Schools the requests for advice and assistance from the Schools Library Services are likely to increase. The main aims of Schools Library Services are to provide services to schools, and professional support to schools and to local education authorities.

INTRODUCTION

The years since the publication of The Library Association's guidelines for school libraries, *Library resource provision in schools* (1977), have been a time of rapid change in education. The great debate on education in 1978 began the process and led to political emphasis on the need to improve standards of education and to involving parents and the community more fully in the education of their children. This has brought forward many educational initiatives, for example: GCSE has replaced GCE 'O' levels and CSE; the Technical and Vocational Education Initiative (TVEI) is changing the approach to learning in secondary schools; the Warnock Report has given emphasis to the needs of children with learning difficulties; the Higginson Report has recommended changes in sixth-form examinations, and the Education, Science and Arts Committee of the House of Commons has recommended the development of education for the under-fives.

For England and Wales the most fundamental changes are contained in the provisions of the Education Reform Act of 1988, most notably the introduction of the National Curriculum and Local Management of Schools (LMS). The Education Reform (Northern Ireland) Order of 1989 has assured similar provision for Northern Ireland through the introduction of the Common Curriculum, but there is as yet no comparable legislation for Scotland. In contrast to the situation in the rest of the UK, Scotland's curriculum development has been characterized by gradual changes achieved through consultation – led by the Scottish Consultative Council on the Curriculum. A 5–14 Development Programme was begun in 1988; the Secretary of State sought to achieve clearer definition of curriculum objectives, development of guidelines on programmes of study and attainment targets, and the introduction of assessment procedures.

A recurring theme in all these new developments is the entitlement of every child to a broad and balanced curriculum designed to meet the individual needs of each child. To achieve curricula of such scope and differentiation, children must be actively involved in their own learning and this requires a shift of emphasis from the learning of facts to the development of skills and an understanding of the processes of learning. As the Library and Information Services Council report, *School libraries: the foundations of the curriculum* states, 'one major thread of a pupil's school life is that of gradually developing the ability to pose questions, to seek sources of information and to select, arrange and present'.[1] The Library and Information Services Council (Scotland) report of 1985 (*Library services and resources for schools in Scotland*) similarly drew attention to the need for children to develop information-handling skills.[2] This in turn requires more detailed curriculum planning and more effective management of resources, and thus creates an increasingly important role for library and information services both within the individual school and in every local education authority.

This new role for school library and information services having been created, it is vital that resources are made available to support them. Her Majesty's Inspectorate (HMI) reports, and more recently monitoring and evaluation in local education authorities, are highlighting both inadequacies and inequalities of school library resource centres – in their staffing, stock and accommodation, and the need to develop the learning and information skills curriculum.

Devolvement of school budgets through LMS may exacerbate the problem. Much development work is needed to ensure that the learning needs of children are effectively supported. It is The Library Association's strongly held view that this will require an effective and well resourced Schools Library Service in every local education authority, to provide the professional expertise and bibliographic support to help schools to achieve the necessary standards for their school library resource centres and to develop their library and information services. These guidelines are needed as never before.

Aims
These guidelines therefore aim to:

10

1 Provide a rationale for school library resource centres and learning resources across the curriculum for the whole of the United Kingdom.
2 Address the need for policies relating to the management of learning resources in schools and LEAs.
3 Outline the implications of a learning skills curriculum.
4 Offer practical guidance on school library resource centre management and the development of an effective library and information service, including staffing, stock, accommodation and funding requirements.
5 Make recommendations to schools, governing bodies, LEAs and government.

Learning resources across the curriculum: context, purpose and function

Context

> The Library is not aside from, or a buttress to, the curriculum, but its skills are the very foundations of the curriculum. (*School libraries: the foundations of the curriculum*, HMSO, 1984).

School libraries must be considered in the context of current work on the curriculum. In the systems of education in this country there has been a significant shift from the priority of content towards the skills and processes of learning. The Government's White Paper *Better schools*[3] and more recent reports, consultation documents and papers have suggested the purpose of learning in primary and secondary schools should be to help pupils to:

- develop lively, enquiring minds;
- question and argue rationally and apply themselves to tasks and physical skills;
- acquire knowledge and skills relevant to adult life and employment in a fast-changing world;
- use language and number effectively;
- respect religious and moral values, and develop tolerance of other races, religions and ways of life;
- understand the world in which they live, and the interdependence of individuals, groups and nations;
- appreciate human achievements and aspirations.

In recent years the Government and Her Majesty's Inspectorate (HMI) have placed emphasis on the need to create more opportunities for pupils to be actively involved in the learning process and to be given scope in their studies to engage in investigative work which requires them to collect, select, organize and present information. The HMI document *The curriculum from 5–16* stated:

A school's curriculum consists of all those activities designed or encouraged within its organisational framework to promote the intellectual, personal, social and physical development of its pupils.[4]

It is recommended that, in designing the curriculum, attention should be paid equally to 'areas of learning and experience' and to 'the elements of learning', i.e. the knowledge, concepts, skills and attitudes to be developed. Some curriculum initiatives have already demonstrated this shift of emphasis. For example, the curriculum of the Certificate of Pre-Vocational Education (CPVE) programme is expressed in a description of skills to be developed and the same is true for much of the work developed in TVEI. The national initiative to develop Records of Achievement also places emphasis on developing and assessing pupils' learning skills. Although GCSE, Scottish Standard Grade, the National Curriculum in England and Wales and the Common Curriculum in Northern Ireland are approached from a subject-related perspective, there is evidence in the criteria for GCSE and Standard Grade that the pupils' ability to be actively engaged in the learning process is as important as their ability to memorize facts. The requirements for the National Curriculum include the teaching of various subjects and themes through the core and foundation subjects, and these will include concepts, skills and attitudes described in *The curriculum from 5–16*.

As the emphasis on the processes of the curriculum and on the development and assessment of pupils' learning skills increases, so does the demand for appropriate resources and facilities to support this. The national criteria for GCSE have assumed an appropriate range of information sources for pupils in order for them to, for example:

- select and present relevant factual information in an organized manner (Religious Education);
- identify and disseminate among differing sources of information (Economics);
- analyse, interpret and draw inferences from a variety of forms of information (Biology).

In the National Curriculum, proposed attainment targets (ATs) will be best supported in those schools which have a broadly balanced and up-to-date provision of learning resources, for example:

the development of the ability to read, understand and respond to all types of writing, as well as the development of information retrieval strategies for the purpose of study (English AT 2 – Reading).

In the context of an extended investigation [pupils should]:

- initiate a piece of self-generated background research employing a variety of resources of information;
- plan a range of exploratory techniques, for example, experiments, literature searches, data logging and analysis (Science AT 1, level 9);
- working to a scheme derived from their previously developed design ... be able to identify, manage and use appropriate resources, including both knowledge and process, in order to make an artefact or system (Design and Technology AT 4).

Purpose
Clearly, therefore, the purpose of school library resource centres and their library and information services provision in schools is wide-ranging.

1 They have a central place in providing a range of information resources in support of the curriculum and of pupils' personal and social development.
2 School library resource centres have been recognized as part of the national information network, contributing to the provision of access to information needed by 'individual citizens if they are to play a full and effective role in society'.[5]

They therefore provide a link between the school and the national information infrastructure.

3   However, simply providing a range of resources in the school is not sufficient: 'any resource is only as good as its real contribution to learning and teaching'.[6] The purpose of the school library resource centre is to facilitate learning and teaching. Steps need to be taken to ensure that library and information services are managed effectively and used fully as an integral part of the curriculum.

Function

Better school library resource centres 'are rooted in the active belief of all staff, clearly stated, that the library is essential to the healthy growth of learning and that the library and its use are the responsibility of all teachers and of all others concerned with promoting learning'.[7] The emphasis on learning to learn, and learning to handle information, so evident in modern curricula,[8] brings library and information services into the centre of the delivery of the curriculum and into the centre of the learning process. The functions of a school library resource centre could therefore be summarized as follows:

1   To assist in providing a comprehensive source of learning materials in different formats for use by pupils individually and in small groups and provide opportunity for loan for home use; to satisfy curricular, cultural and supplementary requirements.

2   To organize all relevant learning and teaching materials within the school, providing a centralized information system concerning all the learning resources available to the school. This should be readily accessible in the school library resource centre.

3   To act as liaison with outside agencies and information sources and encourage their use by pupils and staff.

4   To acquire and disseminate comprehensive information to all staff on materials to meet professional needs and, in co-operation with them, to be actively involved in curricular development within the school as well as maintaining liaison with appropriate bodies in this respect.

5   To make its team available for teachers to consult on the selec-

tion and use of appropriate material to achieve their learning objectives.

6 To make opportunities for staff and pupils to learn how to use relevant materials, and to provide training in the exploitation of the facilities of a school library resource centre. The school library resource centre should provide a focus for the development of the school's information skills curriculum.

The planning of library and information services in schools to fulfil these functions is the subject of these guidelines. The school library resource centre is an essential element in the school's curriculum planning processes and the following chapters will therefore consider how schools may develop and manage their library and information services to meet developing curriculum needs:

1 Management and staffing structures
2 Provision of accommodation
3 Learning resources: their management and organization
4 Learning skills
5 Schools Library Services
Conclusion

References

1 Library and Information Services Council. Working Party on School Library Services, *School libraries: the foundations of the curriculum*, HMSO, 1984.
2 Library and Information Services Council (Scotland), *Library services and resources for Scotland*, Edinburgh, National Library of Scotland, 1985.
3 Department of Education and Science and the Welsh Office, *Better schools*, HMSO, 1985. Cmnd. 9469.
4 Department of Education and Science, *The curriculum from 5–16*, DES, 1985.
5 Office of Arts and Libraries, *The future development of libraries and information services*, HMSO, 1982.
6 Scottish Education Department, *Effective secondary schools*, HMSO, 1988.
7 Department of Education and Science, *Better libraries: good practice in schools*, DES, 1989.
8 Marland, M. (ed.), *Information skills in the secondary curriculum*, Methuen Educational, 1981.

1 MANAGEMENT AND STAFFING STRUCTURES

The learning process
1.1 The emphasis on learning to learn and learning to handle information, so evident in modern curricula, has brought library and information services into the centre of the learning process and reaffirms their essential role in the effective delivery of the curriculum.

Learning skills
1.2 Within each school there should be an appropriate range of cross-curricular learning resources from which pupils can work. Pupils need to develop analytical skills which will help them select from a range of sources, to discriminate between what is relevant and what is not, to interpret the context and draw inferences from it.

1.3 The rapid explosion of sources of information, and the development of technology for the storage and retrieval of data, highlight the necessity to provide pupils with the skills of retrieving and using information effectively, skills that they will use at school and as adults. These need to be developed progressively throughout a pupil's school career, from the reception class to post-16.

Learning resources
1.4 It is essential to have an effective and efficient system for the provision, organization, management and utilization of all the learning resources in a school, as well as awareness of other collections of resources and their systems outside of the school. All schools need to be aware of their requirements for such a system and how that system will be operated for the good of the whole school.

1.5   The most efficient method of ensuring the effective provision of library and information services is by centralizing most of the school's learning resources in the school library resource centre, and providing a centralized information system concerning all the learning resources available to a school.

1.6   The services of professional, chartered librarians trained in the provision, organization, management and utilization of such resources and information are required, to enable such a centralized provision of complex collections of resources and information to be thoroughly effective.

School management structures
1.7   Many secondary schools have in recent years appointed chartered librarians to ensure the effective provision of learning resources across the curriculum. Some secondary schools have also achieved excellent liaison with their feeder schools through their Library and Information Service and by the Librarian working in partnership with teaching colleagues.

1.8   It is less common for primary schools to establish a post for a chartered librarian, although in some parts of the United Kingdom consortia of schools have appointed Chartered Librarians on a shared basis.

1.9   The effective management of such capital-intensive and cross-curricular resources as a library and information service must be of concern to the whole school. The service should therefore be represented in the existing management structure at a senior level. It is only through operating within the management structure at this level and participating in senior management meetings, that the development, implementation and evaluation of school policies can be monitored effectively.

1.10   Appropriate management structures, such as those described in Figs. 1 and 2, should facilitate the collaboration between the Head of Library and Information Services and teaching colleagues. Such collaboration will assist in curriculum planning and development and the management of all learning resources and guidance, and will help to ensure training for all staff and students on the effective use of these learning resources.

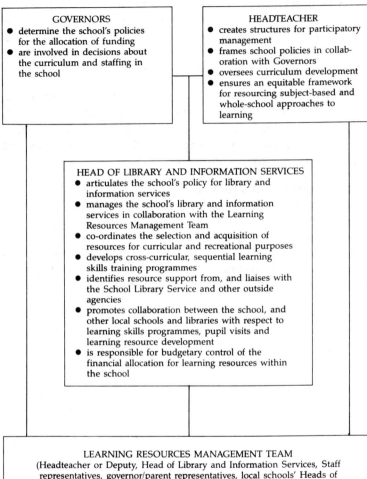

GOVERNORS
- determine the school's policies for the allocation of funding
- are involved in decisions about the curriculum and staffing in the school

HEADTEACHER
- creates structures for participatory management
- frames school policies in collaboration with Governors
- oversees curriculum development
- ensures an equitable framework for resourcing subject-based and whole-school approaches to learning

HEAD OF LIBRARY AND INFORMATION SERVICES
- articulates the school's policy for library and information services
- manages the school's library and information services in collaboration with the Learning Resources Management Team
- co-ordinates the selection and acquisition of resources for curricular and recreational purposes
- develops cross-curricular, sequential learning skills training programmes
- identifies resource support from, and liaises with the School Library Service and other outside agencies
- promotes collaboration between the school, and other local schools and libraries with respect to learning skills programmes, pupil visits and learning resource development
- is responsible for budgetary control of the financial allocation for learning resources within the school

LEARNING RESOURCES MANAGEMENT TEAM
(Headteacher or Deputy, Head of Library and Information Services, Staff representatives, governor/parent representatives, local schools' Heads of Library and Information Service)

- oversees implementation of the school's library and information services policy and monitors its effectiveness and equitability
- seeks a level of funding which ensures the maintenance and development of library and information services to meet the school's needs
- promotes library and information services in the school
- supports the development of curriculum-related learning skills within the school and in relation to learning skills programmes in other local schools
- relates resource selection to the school's curriculum

Fig. 1 Example of a management structure for an individual primary or secondary school's library and information services

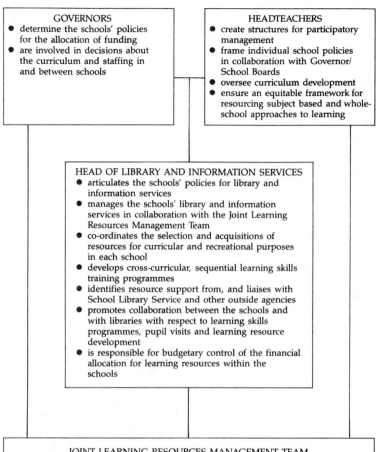

GOVERNORS
- determine the schools' policies for the allocation of funding
- are involved in decisions about the curriculum and staffing in and between schools

HEADTEACHERS
- create structures for participatory management
- frame individual school policies in collaboration with Governor/School Boards
- oversee curriculum development
- ensure an equitable framework for resourcing subject based and whole-school approaches to learning

HEAD OF LIBRARY AND INFORMATION SERVICES
- articulates the schools' policies for library and information services
- manages the schools' library and information services in collaboration with the Joint Learning Resources Management Team
- co-ordinates the selection and acquisitions of resources for curricular and recreational purposes in each school
- develops cross-curricular, sequential learning skills training programmes
- identifies resource support from, and liaises with School Library Service and other outside agencies
- promotes collaboration between the schools and with libraries with respect to learning skills programmes, pupil visits and learning resource development
- is responsible for budgetary control of the financial allocation for learning resources within the schools

JOINT LEARNING RESOURCES MANAGEMENT TEAM
(Headteachers or Deputies, Head of Library and Information Services, Staff representatives, governor/parent representatives)

- oversees implementation of the schools' library and information services policies and monitors their effectiveness and equitability
- seeks a level of funding which ensures the maintenance and development of library and information services to meet each school's needs
- promotes library and information services in the schools
- supports the development of curriculum-related learning skills within and between schools
- relates resource selection to the schools' curricula

Fig. 2   Example of a management structure for library and information services in a consortium of schools

19

Links with associated schools through the Head of Library and Information Services will enable continuity and progression in the learning process to be achieved not only within, but also between schools.

Library and information services

1.11   The educational reasons for the appointment of chartered librarians in schools include:

- the nature and pace of change in the curriculum, which involves a wider use of the full range of learning resources;
- the consequent need of teachers and pupils for assistance and guidance in locating and using resources effectively throughout the school day;
- the need for cross-curricular coordination to provide for the equitable and cost effective distribution and use of resources for all ages and abilities and to facilitate learning;
- the need to promote a cross-curricular and sequential programme of learning skills from reception class to post-16;
- the need to identify resources of information available from outside the school linking in with local, national and international information networks, to support the curriculum.

1.12   As well as offering the kind of collaborative strategies which make for both educational and financial efficiency, Fig. 2 indicates a developmental progression in the consortium model – where the services of a chartered librarian are shared, for example, between local primary schools, or between a small number of primary schools and a local secondary school. In the individual model (Fig. 1) a chartered librarian, as Head of Library and Information Services, works exclusively in one school.

Professional training and skills of chartered librarians

1.13   Librarianship and Information Science is a graduate profession and chartered librarians will have completed either a three-year undergraduate or a one-year postgraduate course in Library and Information Studies. (Courses are accredited by The Library Association.) The courses in Library and Information Studies develop expertise in the management, organization and dissemination of information, in all the varied aspects of the management of Library and Information Services and in the effective use of world-wide library and information networks, both print and computer based. A graduate may then apply to become a candidate for admission to the Register of the Library Association and undergo one year of supervised or two years unsupervised post-qualification training in a Library and Information Service. After this, a detailed professional development report is required by The Library Association before he or she is admitted to the Professional Register.

The role of chartered librarians in schools

1.14 The role of chartered librarians lies within the framework of a whole school resources policy. A librarian should:

- collaborate with teachers and other educationalists in the development and evaluation of pupils' learning skills across the curriculum;
- maximize the effective use of the school's learning resources by the whole school community;
- provide access to a comprehensive range of learning materials in different formats for use by pupils individually and in small groups, selected to satisfy curricular, cultural and individual requirements, and to offer opportunity for borrowing;
- enhance cross-curricular initiatives supporting multi-cultural education and equality for all;
- organize all relevant learning and teaching materials within the school to facilitate their location, accessibility and use;
- maintain up-to-date professional awareness of learning resources availability and use through regular visits to the Schools Library Service, attendance at exhibitions, training sessions and contact with publishers and other resource providers;
- liaise with outside agencies and information networks and encourage their use by pupils and staff in order to extend the range of resources available to the school;
- acquire and disseminate comprehensive information to all staff to meet professional needs, and advise staff on the selection of appropriate material to achieve their learning objectives;

- provide facilities for the production of learning materials within the school by staff and pupils;
- promote and foster the enjoyment of reading from the earliest age and encourage the reading habit and enrichment of pupils' imaginative and creative life at all ages through a variety of resources, taking into account their interests and abilities.

The chartered librarian as Head of Library and Information Services

Experience
1.15 The professional and managerial responsibilities described above require the knowledge, experience and skills of a mature chartered librarian with several years of experience. Both the post and the post holder should be treated on the same basis as a head of teaching faculty in the school in terms of salary, conditions of service and status. The Library Association recommends that a chartered librarian in such a post should, at a minimum, be appointed to grades SO1/SO2 of the National Joint Council for Local Authorities (England and Wales), AP IV/V of the National Joint Council for Local Authorities (Scotland).

Training
1.16 Opportunities for the further professional development and training of Heads of Library and Information Services and other staff in the school library resource centre should similarly be no less favourable than those of their teaching colleagues within schools. This includes participation in professional meetings, in-service training and externally organized courses. Such opportunities help professionals to provide a wider professional experience, benefiting the school as well as the individual.

Personal qualities
1.17 The remit of the Head of Library and Information Services will itself help to define the professional and personal qualities required to be effective. Uppermost is the ability to contribute as an equal, professional partner working as a coordinating member of the learning resources management team.

Dealing with the great variety of people within a school and in the wider community demands effective communication skills, including the ability to articulate clearly, to make and support a case and be assertive when necessary. The cross-curricular nature of the post demands a knowledge of the range of teaching and learning strategies employed in the school, enabling a matching of curricular demands to the appropriate resources.

Support staff

1.18   In order to meet the professional and managerial demands of an effective Library and Information Service, it is essential that full-time assistance is provided to carry out clerical and technical work. These posts should be filled by clerical/technical assistants whose function is to enable the Head of Library and Information Services to fulfil a professional role by undertaking many of the routine tasks necessary for the smooth running of the Library and Information Service, e.g. operating systems for the loan and returning of resources; implementing the acquisition and organization of resources; updating bibliographic and other databases; reprographic work. They also ensure that the day to day running of the Library and Information Service is unimpeded by the Head of the Service's attendance at meetings with senior managers and teaching colleagues, contribution to in-service education and training (INSET) work and visits to other schools as part of the work to ensure continuity between primary and secondary stages.

Support staff posts should be graded to complement the position of the Head of Library and Information Services and to reflect the duties and responsibilities of the particular post. For an Assistant who undertakes the day to day operation of the school library resource centre, an appointment at Grade 3 of the National Joint Council for Local Authorities (England and Wales) or Grade 2/3 of the National Joint Council for Local Authorities (Scotland), would be appropriate.

1.19   In those schools where the curricular demands on Library and Information Services dictate, or where there are separate resource collections in different buildings, more than one chartered librarian will be needed to respond successfully to the increasing requirements of staff and pupils.

1.20   Where additional posts for professional librarians are provided in schools, these could be open to newly qualified librarians who are seeking the necessary experience to fit them eventually for the post of a school's Head of Library and Information Service. Where possible, a person who is still fulfilling the required for chartered status, should be supervised by a chartered librarian and those involved in making his or her appointment should take this into consideration. All professional staff require opportunities for training and development.

1.21 Schools should also consider how they might make provision for the absence of Library and Information Services staff due to sickness, maternity leave, training or other reasons.

(For up to date advice on recommended salary grades and conditions of service for librarians working in schools, see The Library Association's annual Salary Guide for school library staff.)

Recommendations

1.22 **The Library Association recommends that:**

(a) all schools, primary and secondary, should consider the most effective and efficient means of acquiring the skills of chartered librarians to facilitate the utilization, organization and management of their learning resources. The examples of management structures provided in the guidelines should be related to the needs of individual schools.

(b) the effective development, implementation and evaluation of schools' learning resources policies by chartered librarians and the management of capital intensive and cross-curricular resources should be brought into the existing management structures of schools at a senior level.

(c) all schools should consider the additional staffing requirements and conditions of service procedures needed to enable chartered librarians to respond successfully to the increasing curricular demands from staff and pupils. This includes provision for adequate numbers of clerical and technical support staff.

Further reading

Howard, J. and Hopkins, D., *Information skills in TVEI and the role of the librarian*, British Library, 1988 (British Library Research Paper 51).

Irving, A., *The school librarian's day: an investigation into the role and functions of the school librarian through an analysis of the day's work*, British Library, 1986.

Library and Information Services Council. Working Party on School Library Services, *School libraries: the foundation of the curriculum*, HMSO, 1984.

Library Association, *Salary guide: No 9 school library staff*, Library Association. Annual.

Pain, H. and Lesquereux, J., *Implementing a school library policy: the librarian's role*, School Libraries Group of the Library Association, 1987.

Scottish Library Association, *The school library resource service and the curriculum: 'before five' to 'sixteen plus'*, Scottish Library Association, 1985.

Smith, M., Charlton, L. and Springford, P. (eds.), *Learning resources in secondary schools: guidelines for good practice*, Cambridgeshire County Council Education Service, 1988.

Thomson, L. and Meek, M., *Developing resource-based learning – one school's approach*, Longman/SCDC, 1985.

Valentine, P. and Nelson, B., *Sneaky teaching: the role of the school librarian – teachers' and librarians' perceptions*, British Library, 1989.

West Sussex County Council, *Libraries in primary schools – guidelines for development*, West Sussex County Council, 1988.

2 PROVISION OF ACCOMMODATION

Introduction

2.1 Although school building programmes have contracted during the 1980s there have been many school re-organizations and much adaptation of existing buildings. The increasingly important role of school library and information services has been recognized in the large number of new and adapted school library resource centres that have been created in schools in recent years. Some of these have been a part of local education authority (LEA) building programmes, but increasingly, local initiatives and private fund raising have enabled improved library resource centre accommodation to be developed. The introduction of Local Management of Schools is likely to accelerate this process and, as the need for better accommodation for library and information services is urgent in all phases of education, guidelines for this provision are timely.

2.2 Schools Library Service advisory staff have a particularly important role to play in the planning and design of school library resource centres. Their wide knowledge of schools in an authority enables them to provide valuable advice to governors, head teachers, and heads of library and information services in schools; and their technical knowledge is vital to education officers responsible for building development and to architects. Close cooperation between staff in the LEA and staff in schools is needed to ensure efficient and economical use of resources and the provision of effective and well planned library and information services in schools.

2.3 Guidance on school library resource centre accommodation will cover:

Function and use
Siting
Amount of space required
Allocation of space
Furniture and equipment
Administrative accommodation

Function and use

2.4 It is essential that in deciding the arrangements for the accommodation of learning resources in schools account be taken of the way material will be used in teaching and learning. It is now generally recognized that a central organization of library and information resources is necessary in all types of school, to serve as an agency for the selection and use of books and other learning materials by both staff and pupils, and to facilitate the efficient acquisition, maintenance and exploitation of learning resources throughout the school. Such provision does not suggest that the school library resource centre is the only place where books and other learning materials will be found. The resources collection may well be widely dispersed. Attractive book corners, reading bays and displays of books and other materials concerned with activities of current interest in home-bases are extremely important, especially for young children. In this way, the school library resource centre may be envisaged as a pool from which to draw when selecting material for use in the home-bases and other areas of the school. Whatever the size or structure of a school it is absolutely essential that unrelated and unrecorded selections of material are avoided, since they inevitably result in a more limited and unbalanced range of stock, unnecessary duplication, underuse, and, sometimes, inappropriate use of stock.

Siting

2.5 The school's library and information service should be sited in a library resource centre on one floor, easily accessible from as many teaching spaces as possible, but not a means of access between them.

2.6 While the school library resource centre needs to be relatively free from noise, this is less important than its accessibility. It should not be designed for dual use as a classroom because it will be required for library purposes throughout the school day by individuals and groups.

2.7 It is also essential that there is good vehicular access close to the school library resource centre for the delivery of books and other materials and equipment.

Amount of space required

2.8 The following formula for calculating the amount of space required has been based on the space needed to accommodate one-tenth of the pupils of the school, together with the bookstock and other media, furniture, equipment and administrative accommodation recommended in the rest of the guidelines. It is emphasized that this amount of accommodation is the minimum in which it is possible to carry out the functions of the school's library and information service, as set out in paragraphs 2.12 to 2.14. Schools with fewer than 240 pupils should be treated as if they had 240. Space has been calculated as a fixed proportion of the minimum teaching area of the school allowed by the Department of Education and Science. In this way, the size of a school library resource centre will relate to the school's overall provision and thus a fairer proportion of resources will be allocated to it than has been customary in many types of school buildings.

2.9 It is therefore recommended that a formula of 10% of the minimum teaching area be applied.

2.10 Examples of sizes required are based on The Education (School Premises) Regulations 1981 (Statutory Instruments, 1981, No. 909).

Age range	No of pupils	Minimum teaching accommodation, m^2	Amount of library accommodation required (10%), m^2
5–7	240	571	57
5–11	240	595	59
5–12	320	806	80
8–12	320	858	85
9–13	480	1440	144
11–16	600	2574	257
11–18	720	3086	308
12–18	1500	5937	593
16–18	500	2555	255

2.11 Additional library spaces, such as quiet areas or book corners, would normally be considered as part of the classroom or home-base area. Where, however, large schools are accommodated in separate buildings, additional library areas are likely to be necessary, the size of which should be calculated on the number of pupils housed in the separate building. These areas should be considered as part of the total library resource centre for the school.

Allocation of space
2.12 In all school library resource centres space should be included for the following functions:

Books and information materials storage, appraisal and display, including equipment for this;
Catalogues and indexes;
Issue and discharge of books and information materials;
Exhibition of both two- and three-dimensional materials;
Space for individual study and small group work on books and other media, including computers and other equipment, for one-tenth of the pupils of the school.

This is the minimum provision for all types of schools.

2.13 Middle schools should in addition have space for a general work room including secure storage facilities for IT and audiovisual equipment.

2.14 In secondary schools the following additional spaces should be provided:

Advice and information service point
Area for access to databases
Library staff workroom
Planning and preparation unit

Relationships
2.15 It would not be appropriate to lay down precise amounts of space for each individual item listed, since schools' needs will vary and the school library resource centre must be seen in the context of the whole school. There are, however, relationships between certain of the areas noted above: the advice and

information service point should be located near to the catalogues, indexes, databases and the quick reference section, but separate from the issue and discharge of materials. These should all be situated close to the entrance for ease of access and control. Ease of supervision of the whole centre is an important factor in its design.

2.16 In small schools, book storage and display is generally best arranged around the walls, thus leaving floor space for chairs, tables and circulation, so heating and lighting should be planned to give maximum wall space. In larger schools it may be advantageous to break up the space and so leave more wall-space for display. In these larger library resource centres, display facilities and blocks of shelving can be used to break up the areas within the main library, separating, for example, study space from browsing/informal reading space, the former being situated as far as possible from the entrance and the latter opening from it.

Furniture and equipment

Books
2.17 Shelving should be provided for 75% of the school's ultimate bookstock. All shelving must be adjustable and inter-changeable and it should include provision for display of periodicals, videos, paperbacks and books of all sizes. The height of shelving will vary according to type of school.

Recommended overall height of shelving

Wall stacks:	For Secondary School	Max 1950 mm
	For Middle School	Max 1500 mm
	For Primary School	Max 1200 mm
Island stacks:		1200 mm or 1500 mm
Height of bottom shelf from the floor		300 mm
Length of individual shelves		900 mm
Horizontal book shelving		
General fiction and non-fiction stock		175 – 200 mm
Oversize books, reference books and		
music scores (with vertical divisions)		250 mm
Sloping shelving		
Display and periodicals		300 mm

As much display shelving as possible should be included to attract pupils to the materials, but it should be noted that a 900 mm horizontal shelf will hold approximately 30 books. As far as space permits, a third of the shelving in the primary school, a quarter of the shelving in the middle school, and one-sixth of the shelving in the secondary school should be for display.

Guiding Facilities for guiding of tiers and shelves should be provided.

Book supports These are required for each horizontal shelf.

Non-book materials
2.18 Facilities will be required for the storage of non-book materials including pamphlets, maps, clippings, slides, computer software, cassettes and overhead projector transparencies. In considering the methods of storage of non-book materials, account should be taken of degrees of access, suitability for browsing, security, format and special physical conditions needed. Preference should be given to those methods of storage that will enable non-book materials to be collated with books as required and which allow alternative arrangements. Some special storage units will however be required, including:

Cabinets for wall charts, posters and maps;
Filing cabinets for study folders;
Display racks for periodicals.

Expert advice on detailed planning for library and information materials is available locally from the Schools Library Service.

Counter area
2.19 The counter area provides the information and supervision point for the whole school library resource centre. In small schools an ordinary office desk with storage drawers should suffice, while in larger schools specially designed counter units are available from library furniture suppliers or they may be architect designed. The counter unit should be selected for the type of issuing system in use (see paragraph 2.20), the equipment available for the information retrieval (see paragraph 2.21) and the number of staff working at the counter.

Issuing of materials

2.20 In schools issuing only small quantities of books the traditional method, by readers' tickets and bookcards, is likely to remain the most effective and efficient means of recording loans of materials. Where the number of items loaned warrants the expenditure of time and equipment, a computerized system including borrower records, loan records, overdue and request systems, should be introduced. As the number of systems currently available is continually growing and changing, local advice together with commercial information should be sought.

Catalogues and indexes

2.21 In small schools this may consist of a card catalogue cabinet and/or a visual index, both of which can be purchased from specialist firms. Increasingly, however, larger schools are looking to computerized systems, for which local expertise from the Schools Library Service, together with commercial information, can be sought.

Display

2.22 In addition to the provision for display within the main shelving, facilities will be required for more general displays incorporating other materials. These should include pinboard (preferably fabric covered) and special display units where books and other materials may be displayed in either open or securely lockable showcases. These may be immediately outside the school library resource centre (where they may need to be lockable), in the entrance area or forming attractive units within the library resource centre. Display facilities need to be as attractive and as flexible as possible and be well lighted.

Seating and work spaces

2.23 These should be provided in the main library resource centre for one-tenth of the pupils, and include individual and group study spaces as well as informal seating in easy chairs, on small stools, on upholstered benches, on bean bags or scatter cushions. Some individual and group spaces need to be equipped for computer and audiovisual use in purpose-built units, with consideration given to the cabling requirements for computers and audiovisual equipment and a plentiful supply of conveniently situated power points. The majority of work spaces should however be at individual desks and tables for two or four pupils.

Trolleys
2.24 Standard trolleys for books and other materials are also required.

Additional space requirements
2.25 In all schools space is needed to accommodate at least one whole class either within the main library resource centre or close to it. This area should be sited to cause minimum disturbance to other users. In secondary schools an IT room is required: close to the main library resource centre and equipped to take small classes using computers and other information resources. One or more small rooms for tutorial groups and other shared work should also be provided for secondary schools.

Locker facilities and security
2.26 All secondary schools (including middle deemed secondary) need an area close to the entrance of the main library resource centre for pupils to leave their bags and other personal belongings while they are in the library resource centre. This is essential for security of stock. Larger schools might also consider the installation of an electronic security system. Local advice may be sought from the Schools Library Service on the systems available and their costs.

Administrative accommodation

Secondary schools
2.27 Library staff workroom
This requires direct access to the computer area and should not be less than 20 m square. It should include a workbench, sink, storage, shelving, staff desks, filing cabinet, internal and external telephones and power points.

2.20 Planning and preparation room
An area should be provided for teachers to work with the library and information service staff in the preparation of learning materials. The area needs working surfaces for preparation of

layouts and storage for materials. Facilities should also include reprographic equipment, a word processor and printer, typewriter, photocopier and equipment for lettering and graphics.

Other schools
2.29   In middle, special and primary schools a general workroom of not less than 12 m square is required, including as many as possible of the features listed in paragraph 2.27 above. Where this is not possible the minimum provision is a walk-in store room. Cooperative arrangements with nearby secondary schools or teachers' centres for use of their facilities should be developed to help smaller schools.

Signing
2.30   The school library resource centre should be well signed throughout the school, as well as having ample clear guiding within it.

Equipment checklists

Information technology
2.31   Regardless of the size of a school and of other IT equipment in the school, the minimum equipment level in the school library resource centre to enable it to fulfil its role should include:

An online computer facility to access local databases, education services and commercial databases;

CD-ROM workstation (at least one, more as more products become available);

Interactive video to encourage one-to-one or small group inter-activity with a wide range of materials on disk;

Desk-top publishing workstation;

Work-stations where pupils can use software packages, word-process work, use spreadsheets, etc.

Basic checklist of equipment
2.32   Overall, the following equipment is required in a school library resource centre:

Audiovisual
Computers, monitors, printers
Video recorders/interactive equipment
Television monitors
16mm projector
Slide/filmstrip projector
Overhead projector
Projection screen
Audiovisual equipment trolleys
Radio/cassette players
Double radio/cassette player
Recording time switches
Slide viewers
Cassette players and headphones
Headphones
Microfiche readers

Office
Telephone
Book shelving trolleys
Issue equipment
Display equipment
Typewriter
Storage crates
Catalogue cabinet

Reprographics
Printing/duplicating equipment
Photocopier
Word processor and printer
Electric stapler
Spiral binder (or similar binding equipment)

Recommendations

2.33 The Library Association recommends that:

(a) all schools, primary and secondary, should make provision for an easily accessible school library resource centre to provide for the central organization of library and information resources.

(b) the size of a school library resource centre should relate to the school's overall provision, and that a formula of 10% of the minimum teaching area of the school be applied.

(c) space should be allocated for all of the necessary functions of the school library resource centre, with careful account taken of the ways in which materials and equipment are used in teaching and learning.

(d) adequate resources be made available for the purchase and maintenance of the necessary furniture and equipment to facilitate the provision of an effective library and information service. The expansion of media and IT equipment needs should be recognized in the funding allocation to the school's library and information service.

Further reading

Akers, N., *CD-ROM, interactive video and satellite TV in the school library*, Library Association School Libraries Group, 1987.

Department of Education and Science, *Better libraries: good practice in schools*, DES, 1989.

Gilman, J., *Information technology and the school library resource centre*, National Council for Educational Technology, 1983.

Irving, A., *Wider horizons: online information services in schools*, British Library, 1990. (Library and Information Research Report 80).

Library and Information Services Council (Wales), *Libraries in maintained secondary schools in Wales*, Cardiff, LISC (Wales), 1990.

Library Association, *Information technology in schools: memorandum of evidence to the Education, Science and Arts Committee of the House of Commons*, Library Association, 1991.

Matthews, S., *CD-ROMs in school libraries*, British Library, 1990.

Pain, H., *School librarianship in the United Kingdom*, British Library, 1987.

Smith, M., Charlton, L. and Springford, P. (eds.), *Learning resources in secondary schools: guidelines for good practice*, Cambridgeshire County Council Education Service, 1988.

West Sussex County Council, *Libraries in primary schools – guidelines for development*, West Sussex County Council, 1988.

3 LEARNING RESOURCES: THEIR MANAGEMENT AND ORGANIZATION

Definition of resources

3.1 A broad definition of a resource is any material which makes a positive contribution to the learning process. This covers everything from print resources, a collection of interactive video disks and a list of people whose expertise can be called on, to online databanks, CD-ROMs and reprographic and technical support.

3.2 The acquisition and management of learning resources needs to be a feature of the School Plan. The resource budget allocation should be an integral part of the school's annual planning cycle and the range, quality and quantity of learning resources needs to be planned within the whole-school learning skills policy. This ensures a regular review of decisions and can lead to more efficient resourcing of the curriculum.

3.3 Today, all school library resource centre collections should include the rich variety of media available in supporting the curriculum. They may then be fully effective in serving the needs of pupils who have grown up in a society which communicates in a variety of ways.

3.4 Examples of learning resources which would reflect such a philosophy include:

Books and pamphlets
Periodicals and newspapers
Charts and posters
Photographs, postcards and other ephemera
Film/visual material including films, filmstrips, slides, video-
    tapes
Audio-cassettes and records
Multi-media kits incorporating a variety of formats.

3.5 In addition, as we enter the 21st century the growth of new technologies means that a school library resource centre which is charged with the task of educating pupils beyond the year 2000 must give consideration to other formats. Those which are rapidly becoming familiar include:

> Microformats as alternatives to bulky print storage (e.g. census returns and newspapers)
> Satellite and cable TV
> Videotext and teletext
> Online databanks, e.g. Campus 2000
> CD-ROM and compact discs
> Software programmes
> Interactive video

Use of resources
3.6 There is a major shift in the way resources are used. Previously, these resources were within a narrow range, and predominantly text-book based; in many cases they were stored in small departmentally-based or even class-based collections. In the main these were used to support formal teaching situations and their use was mediated by the teaching of English, supporting *ad hoc* project work and providing a facility for recreational reading.

3.7 Now, the curriculum demands that students have direct access to larger quantities of a widening range of resources. Additionally, teachers are being encouraged to use multi-media approaches for teaching and learning and they require access to an ever-increasing range of both hardware and software.

3.8 There is a danger, especially in a period of rapid change, that the design of the curriculum and the acquisition and management of resources may become separated. There are two extremes. At one extreme the contexts and methods of learning are chosen on the basis of the resources immediately available. At the other extreme, course design and planning takes place without due regard to the availability of resources or the skills which students need to use them. Both of these approaches can lead to the development of poorly resourced and sterile learning situations.

3.9   What is required is a balance between these two positions. This would be achieved where resources are chosen by teachers and students because of their relevance and accessibility, and because of the contribution they make to the acquisition of information handling skills. Collaboration between teachers, with their expertise in course design, and librarians, with their wide knowledge of the availability of resources and resource management, offers the best way of achieving this balance.

3.10   In order to ensure that this positive relationship develops, school management teams must build the means to achieving this collaboration into their whole school curriculum planning. The same planning structure should exist at authority level, to ensure that the Schools Library Service is included as part of the main thrust of curriculum design.

Resources selection policy
3.11   The management plan must encourage consultation. If people do not have the time to get together – nothing happens. There needs to be an overall, long term development plan which covers the funding, acquisition, evaluation and selection of resources.

3.12   A selection policy is particularly important, as it provides the validity for the resources base. The selection of resources must respond to the school's curricular priorities and must recognize the differing demands of the subjects. Evaluation is crucial to selection.

3.13   Information resources should be evaluated against a set of educational criteria which examines such aspects as learning skills, learning outcomes, appropriateness, differentiation and bias.

3.14   The quality and quantity of imaginative literature and the role it plays in the overall broad curricular aims of the school would, of course, be a prime consideration within the resources selection policy. This is particularly so for the primary school age group. The younger the age of the pupil the more important a large selection of such titles becomes. Once pupils have mastered the mechanics of reading, their appetite for new books is likely to become voracious. If the school library resource centre is going to play its full part in creating capable and enthusiastic readers it will need to have sufficient and carefully selected stock.

3.15 The English in the National Curriculum document stresses that Key Stage 1 requires 'a range of rich and stimulating texts ... should include picture books, nursery rhymes, poems, folk tales, myths, legends ...'. Pupils 'should experience a wide range of children's literature'.

3.16 The History in the National Curriculum document further demonstrates the range of resources which will be required to deliver the National Curriculum. The Programme of study for Key Stage 1 states: 'Pupils should be helped to develop an awareness of the past through stories from different periods and cultures, including:

- well-known myths and legends;
- stories about historical events;
- eyewitness accounts of historical events;
- fictional stories set in the past.'

3.17 The Programmes of study for Key Stages 1–4 all state: 'Pupils should have opportunities to learn about the past from a range of historical sources, including:

- artefacts;
- pictures and photographs;
- music;
- adults talking about their own past, oral accounts;
- written sources;
- buildings and sites;
- computer based materials.'[2]

3.18 Similar considerations should apply in relation to the curriculum in Scotland and in Northern Ireland. The 5–14 Development Programme for the Scottish curriculum makes an equally strong case for the provision of adequate and carefully selected resources.[3] The Common Curriculum for Northern Ireland, which includes as areas of study: Creative and Expressive Studies; The Environment and Society; Mathematics; English; and a Language, also requires a wide range of carefully selected resources.[4]

Selection criteria

3.19 The following are crucial factors within the resources selection policy:

- the relationship between the curriculum and the resources;
- the appropriateness of the resources to the pupils' abilities and interests;
- the currency of resources;
- the range of available media;
- the contribution resources make to the development of process skills, e.g. information retrieval.

Quantifying the need

3.20 Following an examination of the school's curriculum and resources policies there are a number of models which can be used to help quantify the school's learning resource needs.

3.21 Despite the limitations of quantitative guidelines in reflecting variations between schools in such matters as teaching styles and learning strategies; ability levels of pupils; local background and past provision; such guidelines can usefully provide a template against which the needs of individual schools may be matched.

3.22 However, the number of books and other materials is only one measure of the adequacy of a school library resource centre. The quality, range, condition and match of materials to the pupils and the curriculum are also of crucial importance. For example, an apparently well stocked library resource centre may be found, upon examination, to contain a high proportion of items which are unrelated to the current curriculum or in such poor condition as to be unusable.

3.23 In order to avoid such a situation, every school needs to formulate a clear financial plan which establishes targets for the development and resourcing of its school library resource centre, rather than relying on unspecific estimates of what is needed or can be afforded.

3.24 It is only through regular recognition of the real level of resourcing requirements, based on the policy for the library resource centre, that decisions on the funding requirements of schools can include a realistic assessment of the cost of providing an adequate school library resource centre. If a school only funds its library resource centre on the basis of what is judged affordable, then Heads and Governors are often surprised when the results of that decision are analysed.

3.25 For example, if with an annual budget of £600 a school purchased 100 items (i.e. an average cost of £6 per item) to add to the library resource centre stock of 3,000 relevant items, then the simple calculation of dividing the total stock by the total purchases will show how long each item must last before it can be replaced. The calculation for the above example is:

$$\frac{\text{existing stock}}{\text{no. of items bought this year}} = \frac{3,000 \text{ items}}{100} \quad \text{thus} \quad \text{every item must last for 30 years}$$

Clearly, library resource centre stock, two-thirds of which is between 10 and 30 years old is unlikely to engender much interest in the pupils.

Developing a financial plan for resourcing the school library

3.26 There are a number of preparatory steps to be undertaken in drawing up a financial plan:

1 Assess current provision by determining the number of relevant items in the library resource centre. This constitutes the base stock.
2 Measure the resulting figure against the needs identified in the whole school policy.

The following models are designed to help at this stage to quantify these needs and identify any shortfall.

3 Use the formulae which follow the models to identify the cost of both maintaining the existing stock and increasing stock so as to eliminate the shortfall over a specified period of time. The resulting estimates are described as the Maintenance Budget and the Development Budget.

All these processes are described more fully in the following paragraphs.

Assessing the stock

3.27 Examine the stock and judge its relevance to the curriculum, appropriateness for the ages and abilities of the pupils and its currency and physical condition. If the stock is large, perhaps 13,000 or more items, this could be done on a sampling basis, examining say 1 item in 10. Count the number of items found to be relevant and useful but exclude any Schools Library Service stock. Exclude as well all textbooks, i.e. materials dedicated to structured courses such as reading schemes or language courses, as such items do not normally form part of a library resource centre collection. The resulting figure is the base stock figure which has to be maintained annually and from which to develop.

3.28 HMI assume the active life of a resource item to be 10 years and this should be regarded as the maximum lifespan for all except archive material. Subject areas like Science/Technology/Computers and materials such as paperbacks and picture books will, of course, need earlier replacement.

3.29 The expected lifespan of items provided in the primary school will be less than that in the secondary school, through greater wear and tear in the handling of books and other materials by pupils. Consequently, a lifespan of seven years should be regarded as the maximum.

Model 1 – Minimum provision

3.30 A model of minimum provision based on the National Curriculum (NC) for England and Wales, on the Development Programme for the Scottish Curriculum or the Common Curriculum for Northern Ireland, may provide the most useful starting point for many schools.

Secondary schools

3.31 For example, in English and Welsh secondary schools there are 11 mandatory subjects within the NC (including Religious Education) to be studied by all pupils. The provision of one item per pupil per subject with the addition of two extra items per pupil to meet their personal, recreational and social needs, gives a total of 13 items per pupil as the absolute minimum size of stock to meet current needs.

Example
Number of pupils on roll = 800
No of items per pupil for NC = 800 × 11 = 8,800
No of additional items per student = 800 × 2 = 1,600
Therefore minimum provision = 10,400 items

Thus, in a school where the base stock has been assessed as 7,000 the shortfall identified = 3,400 items.

Primary schools
3.32 For example, in English and Welsh primary schools (i.e. pupils up to the age of 11) there are 10 mandatory subjects in the NC (including Religious Education) and again one item per pupil per subject should be provided. The demands placed on stock during the period when children are learning to read requires that an additional three items are provided to reflect the important role of imaginative literature for this age group. Thus a total of 13 items per pupil is the absolute minimum size of stock to meet current needs.

Example
Number on roll = 200
Number of items per pupil for NC = 200 × 10 = 2,000
No of additional items per pupil = 200 × 3 = 600
Therefore minimum provision = 2,600 items

Thus in a school where the base stock has been assessed at 1,600 the shortfall identified = 1,000 items.

Middle schools
3.33 Minimum provision for middle schools can be calculated from the above figures according to the age of the pupils concerned.

Example
Number on roll = 120 (9–11 year olds)
Number on roll = 180 (12–13 year olds)
No of items per pupil for NC (primary) = 120 × 10 = 1,200
(secondary) = 180 × 11 = 1,980
No of additional items p.p. (primary) = 120 × 3 = 360
(secondary) = 180 × 2 = 360
Therefore minimum provision = 3,900 items.

Model 2 – More effective provision

3.34   For some schools the use of these minimum standards will not provide a stock that fully meets the needs of the school policy, particularly in respect of offering both breadth and depth in the collection and in providing an up-to-date stock in good physical condition that meets the needs of all pupils. These schools may consequently wish to proceed from minimum provision towards a level that could be deemed to be more effective. A model of a more effective provision could be based on the need to meet the demands of the 30% of school time not allocated to the NC. This would allow the collection to develop to provide a breadth and depth of resources capable of responding to the full range of curricular demands from staff and pupils. This model also provides for more regular replacement of stock.

3.35   However, since, in the more enriched stock, it is more likely that around 10% of the materials meet overlapping subject needs because they are cross-curricular in nature this model uses an increase on the minimum provision of 20% not 30%.

Secondary school example
3.36
   Number on roll = 800
   Minimum provision = 10,400
   More effective provision = 10,400 + 20% = 13,000
   (i.e. an increase from 13 items p.p. to 16)

Lifespan of stock should be calculated at between five and seven years depending on the subject area and fragility of the material.

Primary school example
3.37
   Number on roll = 200
   Minimum provision = 2,600
   More effective provision = 2,600 + 20% = 3,250
   (i.e. an increase from 13 items p.p. to 16)

Lifespan of stock should be calculated at between four and six years depending on the topic and the fragility of the material.

Adjustments

3.38 Clearly, these figures are most helpful to schools of average size and with the minimum of special circumstances. Adjustments may need to be considered to meet specific needs. For example:

- *Sixth Form Colleges and Centres* A straight per capita figure based on the NC is clearly inappropriate post–16. The high demand on resources created by the wide curriculum offered to a comparatively small group of students requires a stock of not less than 10,000 items which, in terms of student numbers, might be between 20 and 25 items per student. However, the note on large schools given below might also be relevant.

- *Rural schools* Primary and secondary schools situated in rural areas far from library services which pupils can use to supplement the school stock may need to regard the model for more effective provision as a minimum level necessary to meet their needs.

- *Special needs* Children with special needs, whether as the result of mental or physical disability or of learning difficulties, need to have access to learning resources selected to meet their needs. This is rarely possible within the limitations of a minimum collection.

- *Small schools* When calculating stock provision, experience has shown that schools with fewer than 200 pupils should be provided for as if they were of this size, and this has been recognized by Government when advising on the Local Management of Schools. Smaller collections will not be sufficient in quantity and range to meet the varying interest and ability ranges of pupils or to cover the field of knowledge adequately.

- *Large schools* Large schools have particular problems in responding to quantitative guidelines based on our per capita calculations. A per capita approach can make the minimum levels of provision difficult to meet and, if followed pro-rata, can result in unnecessarily high targets.

3.39 In secondary schools with a pupil population of more than 1,100, economies of scale can be achieved and the previous models could be modified so that the minimum library stock is deemed to be 14,000 items and more effective provision 16,800 items. An increase of library resource centre stock beyond these figures is likely to be counter-productive because of the difficulties pupils would experience in locating relevant material in such a large collection.

3.40 In primary schools of more than 500 pupils, the previous models could be modified so that the minimum stock is deemed to be 6,500 and more effective provision 7,800.

Calculating the cost

3.41 The models above enable a school to establish where it is at present and to set targets for the development of the school library resource centre to meet current and future needs over a period of time. These targets will need to be expressed in terms of costs, and the sum required each year for the purchase of library resource materials will need to be based on a combination of two calculations.

3.42 The first is the maintenance budget which is the sum required to maintain the existing or base stock at its current level, bearing in mind the replacement models provided.

3.43 The second calculation is the development budget which is the sum required each year to eliminate the shortfall and enable the school to proceed towards its target for library resource centre provision.

3.44 In order to determine these amounts, it is necessary first to determine the average price per item of stock. Since there are no nationally accepted average prices for resource materials, advice on expenditure may be sought from the local Schools Library Service on its budget calculations. Schools can also use their own figures from the previous year's expenditure, updated for inflation.

3.45 To calculate the average price per item, the previous year's expenditure is divided by the number of items purchased and then an amount for inflation is added. Comparison between school and Schools Library Service figures will help to ensure realistic average prices.

3.46 The resulting average price per item can then be used in calculating library resource centre budget requirements using the following formulae:

No. of items to be replaced annually	×	Average item price (AIP)	=	Annual maintenance budget

No. of additional items needed to reduce shortfall	×	AIP	=	Annual development budget

Secondary school example
3.47

Number on roll = 800
Base stock = 7,000 items including 1,000 items on loan from Schools Library Service therefore:

School base stock to be maintained = 6,000 items
Minimum stock model target = 10,400 (shortfall = 3,400)
More effective model target   = 13,000 (shortfall = 6,000)

This school has decided to aim for the minimum stock target initially, which requires a replacement of 10% of base stock annually (lifespan of 10 years per item).

The school has calculated the average item price = £8.00. They apply the maintenance budget formula as follows:

Items to be replaced 600	×	AIP £8.00	=	Maintenance budget £4,800.00

The school aims to reach the minimum stock target of 10,400 items over five years. This requires them to budget to add 680 items each year. They apply the development budget formula as follows:

Items to be added 680	×	AIP £8.00	=	Development budget £5,440.00

Therefore total annual budget required on AIP of £8.00 is:

Maintenance budget £4,800.00	+	Development budget £5,440.00	=	£10,240.00 p.a. + inflation

Primary school example
3.48
Number on roll = 200
Base stock = 2,800 items, including 800 items on loan from the Schools Library Service, therefore:

School base stock to be maintained = 2,000 items
Minimum stock model target = 2,600 (no shortfall)
More effective stock model target = 3,250 (shortfall = 450)

This school wishes to achieve the more effective model target and plans to replace 20% of its base stock items annually (lifespan of five years per item).

Because of the proportion of fiction bought in paperback the school calculates the average item price = £6.00.

They apply the maintenance budget formula as follows

Items to be replaced		AIP		Maintenance budget
400	×	£6.00	=	£2,400.00

The school aims to reach the more effective stock target over five years which requires the addition of 90 items annually.

They apply the development budget formula as follows:

Items to be added		AIP		Development budget
90	×	£6.00	=	£540.00

Therefore total annual budget required on AIP of £6.00 is:

Maintenance budget		Development		£2.940.00 p.a.
£2,400.00	+	budget	=	+ inflation
		£540.00		

3.49 An item is a unit of stock packaged in one piece. A 12-volume encyclopaedia counts as 12 items; a set of slides in a wallet, or a topic file of cuttings, each count as one item. To determine how many 'items' a newspaper subscription or subscription to a database is equivalent to, divide the annual cost of the subscription by the average price per item of library resource centre materials. For example, if the average purchase price per item is £6.00, a subscription price of £240.00 counts as 40 items.

Organization
3.50 To ensure their efficient use throughout the school, all learning resources should be organized in a logical way.

3.51 When considering the initial cataloguing and classification of the resource collections it is strongly recommended that standard practices and schemes be adopted as far as possible, albeit with minor adaptations if necessary, so that maximum advantage may be taken of local or national resource agencies. Standardization also makes it simpler to integrate material borrowed from outside sources.

3.52 Such organization will vary in degree and complexity according to the size and type of the school. Computerized systems are playing an increasing part in the organization of information resources and there are a number of systems available, which range from basic versions suitable for use in primary schools to more sophisticated versions for the largest secondary school. As the number and kinds of systems currently available is continually changing and developing, local advice should be sought from Schools Library Service staff.

3.53 Whether a school opts for such a system will be affected by the expertise of the staff, the availability of clerical assistance, finance for hardware and software, etc. However, a central record of all the learning resources, wherever these are sited within the school, should be regarded as essential.

3.54 In addition, there needs to be appropriate labelling and guiding of materials so as to facilitate the retrieval of information. All these aspects need to be considered alongside the school's learning skills policy.

Access
3.55 In order to facilitate the maximum possible use of the school's learning resources, the school library resource centre should be available for staff and pupils' use throughout the school day. As stated in Chapter 2, paragraphs 5–7, careful siting of a library resource centre is an important means of enhancing access. Equally, care must be taken to ensure resources are obtainable whenever teachers and pupils require them.

Recommendations

3.56 **The Library Association recommends that:**

(a) the acquisition and management of learning resources should be a feature of the School Plan, with the resource budget allocation for the school library resource centre an integral part of the school's annual planning cycle.

(b) there should be an overall, long term development plan which covers the funding, acquisition, evaluation and selection of resources; a selection policy is particularly important, as it provides the validity for the resources base.

(c) all school library resource centre collections should include the range of media available for supporting the curriculum.

(d) the quantitative guidelines provided here should be used as a template against which the needs of individual schools can be matched.

(e) resources should be logically organized and with sufficient access to them, in order to facilitate maximum use by pupils and staff.

References

1 Department of Education and Science, *English in the National Curriculum*, DES, 1989, 14.

2 Department of Education and Science, *History in the National Curriculum*, DES, 1991, 13.

3 Scottish Consultative Council on the Curriculum, *Curriculum design for the secondary stages: guidelines for teachers*, Dundee: SCCC, 1989.

4 Northern Ireland Department of Education, *The Education Studies Reform (Northern Ireland) Order, 1989*, Belfast, HMSO, 1989. (SI 1989 24060 NI).

Further reading

Department of Education and Science, *Better libraries: good practice in schools*, DES, 1989.

Department of Education and Science, *Secondary school library survey*, DES, 1981.

Department of Education and Science, *A survey of secondary school libraries in six local education authorities*, DES, 1985 and 1990.

Devon Education/Devon Libraries, *Resources for learning*, Devon County Council, 1990.

Education Publishers Council, *The book check action file: guidelines for governors and teachers in primary schools*, Publishers Association, 1989; *The book check action file: guidelines for governors and teachers in secondary schools*, Publishers Association, 1989.

Griffiths, V. (ed.), *The resource implications of GCSE*, Youth Libraries Group of the Library Association, 1989.

Library and Information Services Committee (Scotland), *Library services and resources for schools education in Scotland*, Edinburgh, National Library for Scotland, 1985.

Library and Information Services Council (Wales), *Libraries in maintained secondary schools in Wales*, Cardiff, LISC (Wales), 1990.

Lincoln, P., *The learning school*, The British Library, 1987. (Library and Information Research Report 62).

National Council for Educational Technology, *Information pack for school librarians*, NCET, 1990.

School Library Association, *Steps in the right direction*, Swindon, SLA, 1989.

Scottish Library Association, *The school library resource and the curriculum: 'before five' to 'sixteen plus'*, Scottish Library Association, 1985.

Smith, M., Charlton, L. and Springford, P. (eds.), *Learning resources in secondary schools: guidelines for good practice*, Cambridgeshire County Council Education Service, 1988.

4 LEARNING SKILLS

The learning skills curriculum

4.1 At the heart of any pupil-centred·learning activity is a sequence of tasks requiring pupils to locate, select, interrogate, interpret and communicate knowledge and understanding. The progressively complex and sophisticated skills needed by pupils to complete these tasks form the learning skills curriculum.

4.2 The use of learning resources needs to be planned within a whole-school learning skills policy which is delivered through the curriculum of each department in secondary schools and by every class-teacher in primary schools.

Today's school children will one day be responsible for creating the nation's wealth and organising its society. An ability to learn throughout life will be crucial in equipping them not only to contribute to the industrial life of the nation but to find happiness themselves and contribute to that of others. It is widely recognised that they must learn how to learn. A central feature of the learning process is learning to deal with information. Information exists in increasing quantity and comes from a variety of sources through an ever increasing range of media. An ability to cope with these changing circumstances is not innate, it must be acquired.[1]

Development of learning skills programmes

4.3 Learning skills, like all other skills, need to be learned and practised. Their acquisition requires a developmental programme following the continuum of education from the infants' school, through the junior school years to the secondary school and into further and higher education. Many learning skills are closely linked to language and reading development and need to be introduced at an appropriate stage, then practised, reinforced and extended. As noted in earlier chapters, the National Curriculum for England and Wales, the Common Curriculum for Northern Ireland and the 5–14 Development Programme for the Scottish Curriculum, together with other innovatory curriculum developments, all point to the significance of appropriate learning skills at every stage in education.

4.4 Every school will need to carry out a regular curriculum audit by closely scrutinizing the curriculum and syllabuses for each subject. This audit will identify those learning skills that need to be acquired at each stage in a child's school career. The chartered librarian designated Head of Library and Information Services will play a key role in this cross-curricular audit.

4.5 Traditionally, library skills, user education and information skills sessions concentrated on finding information – with little emphasis on defining what information was required or how to use and evaluate it effectively. In recent years, chartered librarians have collaborated with teaching staff to introduce cross-curricular training in this much broader area of learning skills.

4.6 The learning skills identified in the new curricula and which form the basis for enquiry framework and research steps listed in recent publications, are as follows:

Planning
Locating and gathering
Selecting and appraising
Organizing and recording
Communicating and realizing
Evaluating

The chartered librarian, as the school's learning resources specialist, in collaboration with all teachers, can ensure that pupils of all abilities are provided with resources to enable them to acquire these skills and with the opportunities, integral to the curriculum, to practise them. The Library Association believes that school library resource centres should be in the charge of a chartered librarian, who as Head of Library and Information Services will have an appropriate salary, conditions of service and status. This is explained more fully in Chapter 1.

Planning skills

4.7 Planning skills are the essential prerequisite for any research task, assignment, project, essay or topic. The chartered librarian plays an indispensable part in this planning process, advising both staff and pupils of resource availability, and thus the viability of any assignment, at the very beginning of the learning process. Brainstorming, appropriate question framing and keyword identification are essential skills that require practice at the planning stage of the learning process.

Locating and gathering skills

4.8 Locating and gathering information for course work assignments, problem solving exercises and other learning activities are fundamental skills, which are too often assumed, yet require practice at increasingly sophisticated levels. An understanding of alphabetical order and numerical order, and the tracking down of source material from other library and information services, organizations, computer databases and people outside school, require expert guidance and advice and appropriate opportunities for practice.

Reinforcement is required of these locating skills; they need to be related to the whole curriculum and developed within a subject context. This will involve the use of indexes, a wide variety of reference sources and the full range of information technologies; from video, videotex and interactive video to online databases, CD-ROM and satellite television. Methods of generating information by survey, interview, experiment or observation, or by using prior knowledge, also need to be practised.

Selecting and appraising skills

4.9 Pupils need to develop critical, evaluative thinking skills. They need guidance from the chartered librarian in learning how to identify relevant, up-to-date and authoritative information, available within school or from outside sources, and in detecting any bias or inaccuracy. A wide range of resources needs to be consulted, compared and appraised, to ensure that hypotheses and conclusions are formed upon the widest possible knowledge base.

Organizing and recording skills

4.10 Dealing with the information that has been gathered and selected also requires the guidance of the chartered librarian, who is trained in the management and use of all information, including audiovisual and other information technologies and in methods of organizing information. Alternative processes of note-taking (using diagrams, audio or video recordings or photography, for example), and of storing information (using cards, files or computerized technologies) need to be learned alongside traditional skills such as summarizing, citing of quotations and tabulation of results. The organization of any assignment, in whatever format, requires an understanding of structural conventions such as headings, chapters and references. The maintenance of full and accurate bibliographies is an essential skill that also needs to be practised in all research situations from an early age.

Communicating and realizing skills

4.11 Communicating the results of the enquiry stages outlined above, or realizing a design in any practical subject in a way that demonstrates a true understanding and interpretation of the information which has been recorded, is one of the most difficult learning skills. Chartered librarians are all too aware of the potential for plagiarism and, with teaching colleagues, have initiated alternative approaches to the presentation of information, from audio and video recordings to computerized databases, as alternatives to rather than replacements for the written word.

Such is the success of these alternative approaches that examiners in many subject areas now accept assignments in any format. However, opportunities to practise and develop skills in the use of these information technologies are required at an early stage in pupils' school careers. The emphasis on the realization of original work in practical subjects is further evidence of the importance attached to these skills in modern curricula.

Evaluating skills

4.12 Evaluating the learning process, the information content and its form of presentation is an equally important stage of any assignment. Relating the finished product to the original plan, determining the strengths and weaknesses of the learning process and reflecting on improvements and implications for any future assignments are essential considerations for the pupil, the teaching staff and the chartered librarian.

4.13 All of these skills need to be introduced, practised and developed in the widest possible range of subject contexts and age phases. Modern curricula demand that a wide variety of methods, both print and technology based, should be used – with pupils working both on their own and in different group sizes. Chartered librarians are not confined to any one subject area, and have expertise in matters relating to information and information handling, learning resources and the learning process. Thus they are able to maintain an overview of the development of learning skills in the school.

4.14 Where suitable linkages have been forged with associated schools, chartered librarians are able to ensure that these skills are developed as part of a sequential programme and introduced to pupils at the appropriate time in their school careers.

Recommendations

4.15 **The Library Association recommends that**:
(a) every school, primary and secondary, should plan the delivery of the learning skills curriculum within a whole-school learning skills policy, identifying those skills applicable to them by means of a regular curriculum audit.
(b) learning skills should be developed as part of a sequential programme, introduced at an appropriate stage and then practised, reinforced and extended in all areas of the curriculum.
(c) learning skills development should involve the chartered librarian as Head of Library and Information Services working in collaboration with teaching colleagues to provide cross-curricular training opportunities in all aspects and stages of the learning process.
(d) the full range of resources and information sources should be used in this learning skills training to satisfy the demands of modern curricula.

References

1 Library and Information Services Council. Working Party on School Library Services, *School libraries: the foundations of the curriculum*, HMSO, 1984.

Further reading

Bradford Education Library Service, *The effective junior and middle school library: a guide to its planning, policy, management and monitoring*, Bradford, City of Bradford Metropolitan Council, 1990.

Carter, C. and Monaco, J., *Learning information technology skills*, British Library, 1987 (Library and Information Research Report 54).

Department of Education and Science, *Better libraries: good practice in schools*, DES, 1989.

Galpin, B. and Schilling, M., *Computers, topic work and young children: learning to use information in the primary classroom*, British Library, 1988.

Gawith, G., *Library alive! promoting reading and research in the school library*, A & C Black, 1987.

Griffiths, V. (ed.), *The resource implications of GCSE*, Youth Libraries Group of The Library Association, 1989.

Howard, H. and Hopkins, D., *Information skills in TVEI and the role of the librarian*, British Library, 1988.

Howard, J., *Information skills and the secondary curriculum: some practical approaches*, British Library, 1991 (Library and Information Research Report 84).

Irving, A., *Wider horizons: online information services in schools*, British Library, 1990 (Library and Information Research Report 80).

Kinnell, M. and Pain-Lewins, H. (eds.), *School libraries and curriculum initiatives*, Taylor Graham, 1988 (British Library Research and Development Report 5969).

Library Association, *General Certificate of Secondary Education: guidance note on the role of libraries, learning resources and librarians*, Library Association, 1988.

Library Association, *National curriculum and assessment*, Library Association, 1992 (Curriculum guidance).

Library Association, *National curriculum and learning skills*, Library Association, 1991 (Curriculum guidance).

Library Association, *Technical Vocational Education Initiative: guidance note on the role of libraries, learning resources and librarians*, Library Association, 1988.

Lincoln, P., *The learning school*, British Library, 1987 (Library and Information Research Report 62).

Markless, S. and Lincoln, P. (eds.), *Tools for learning: a framework of skills*, British Library, 1987 (British Library Research and Development Report 5892).

Pain, H. and Lesquereux, J., *Developing a policy for a school library*, School Libraries Group of The Library Association, 1987.

Pain, H. and Lesquereux, J., *Implementing a school library policy: the librarian's role*, School Libraries Group of The Library Association, 1987.

Pain, H. and Lesquereux, J., *The library and the curriculum*, School Libraries Group of The Library Association, 1988.

Pain-Lewins, H. *et al.*, *Resourcing GCSE*, British Library, 1989. (British Library Research Paper 58).

Scottish Library Association, *The school library resource service and the curriculum: 'before five' to 'sixteen plus'*, Scottish Library Association, 1985.

Smith, M., Charlton, L. and Springford, P. (eds.), *Learning resources in secondary schools: guidelines for good practice*, Cambridgeshire County Council Education Service, 1988.

5 SCHOOLS LIBRARY SERVICES

Introduction

5.1 The decade of the 1980s was significant for the development of curriculum initiatives and of school library resource centres. As was shown in earlier chapters, national concern about the position of school libraries, made clear by the Library and Information Services Council and Her Majesty's Inspectorate, resulted in many local education authorities examining their own provision of library and information services in schools. This led to the creation of policy documents and advances in the staffing and resourcing of school library resource centres. Curriculum changes, particularly in the secondary phase, challenged many schools to review resources management and consequently to recruit chartered librarians to supply the expertise that was previously lacking.

5.2 Furthermore, the learning resource needs of nursery, infant and primary schools also expanded markedly during this period. The variety of approaches to the acquisition of reading, the editing and review process occasioned by *Education for all,*[1] and post-Swann policies, as well as a more sophisticated use of learning resources in the primary curriculum, have kept the school library resource centre firmly in focus.

5.3 The process of development has been guided and supported by Schools Library Services. In England and Wales, these are traditionally operated by the Library Departments of local authorities as agents of the Education Authority, and until the implementation of the 1988 Education Reform Act the Inner London Education Authority provided a schools library support service to schools in the Inner London Boroughs. Since the Education Reform Act, Inner London Boroughs have taken over responsibility for their education services and many of them are now developing their Schools Library Services, either as part of the Library Department, or run under the auspices of Education. In Northern Ireland, Schools Library Services are statutory services within each of the five Education and Library Boards and in Scotland Schools Library Services have usually been placed with the Education Departments, which are administered regionally. The knowledge and experience of chartered librarians in such services have provided elected members and officers with advice and direction. At the same time, professional support, training and resources have been made available to schools in order that pupils derive maximum benefit from their educational experience.

5.4   As the 1990s unfold, the Education Reform Act is likely both to sustain and undermine the advances of the 1980s. Curriculum changes across the UK are already proving an enormous stimulus, and a strain as far as school library resource centre use and resourcing are concerned. Most primary schools could not cope with the demands of the science curriculum alone. As schools meet the challenge of Local Management of Schools (LMS) the requests for advice and assistance for the Schools Library Services are likely to increase.

5.5   Nevertheless, contracting budgets and LMS present a threat to the future of Schools Library Services. Local authority commitment to the retention of the existing services is apparently strong. Yet the realities of a contracting centralized education budget in which a variety of services vie for survival cannot be denied. It is in this context that the time appears appropriate to examine the particular strengths of Schools Library Services, and provide guidelines for their operation.

Rationale
5.6   No library contains all the resources that its clients will require. Such a statement is particularly relevant to school library resource centres, in all phases of education. The wide range of educational and recreational demands their users will make across the ability spectrum, the quantities of materials required and the often extended loan periods involved, as well as the short term needs for specific areas of the curriculum, are factors which

combine to make the school library resource centre unviable as a self-sufficient agency.

5.7 Most local education authorities have recognized that to function effectively for the personal and educational development of pupils, school library resource centres need the support of a specialist library service. As a result, an authority-wide service has been provided which acts as a support, consultancy, training and information network for all local education authority maintained schools. Schools Library Services are the most economic means of providing a wide range of support materials and professional advice. Books, audiovisual resources, computer software and CD-ROM should form the core stock of an effective resources base for school library resource centre provision to schools. There are economies of scale to be gained from providing some of these centrally through a Schools Library Service.

5.8 As the pressure of curriculum change and the demands of the Education Reform Act make increasing demands on the school library resource centre, the benefits of a well organized Schools Library Service become increasingly apparent.

Aims
The main aims of the Schools Library Service are to provide:

5.9 *Services to schools*
- access to loan materials which supplement the core collection for school library resource centres.
- the opportunity to exchange those materials on a regular basis.
- materials which are borrowed by schools for a specific period of time to support project or topic work taking place within the curriculum, but which cannot be sustained by a school's existing resources.
- access to bibliographical information which would be unavailable or financially unsupportable in an individual school library resource centre.
- access to databases and IT support.
- display materials, exhibitions and support for special events

such as book weeks, author visits and other such promotional events.

- a major contribution to materials selection in schools. This may be through a permanent exhibition collection of recommended materials or through specially created collections of materials aimed at the needs of an individual school. Increasingly, primary schools are using in-service training days as an opportunity to invite the Schools Library Service to lead the whole staff in an examination of the school's resources, their relevance and use. Such activities, allied to short course provision, review groups and exhibitions improve the quality of selection of resources by schools and lead inevitably to an improvement in the use of resources.

5.10 *Professional support to schools*

- advisory support to heads, governors, teachers and parents on the management, organization and development of learning resources within schools.
- advice to heads and governors on the recruitment and selection of library resource centre staff in schools.
- professional guidance, counselling and development of library resource centre staff in schools. (This is a complex task, as the people involved encompass parent helpers, clerical assistants, teachers and chartered librarians. The experience and abilities of library resource centre workers from such diverse backgrounds demand a flexible, discerning and highly professional range of support strategies.)
- support to schools on the processes of performance measurement as applied to school library resource centres, and assistance for schools in the development of performance indicators.
- advice for staff with library resource centre responsibility on the development of budget bids and the presentation of regular reports to heads and governors.
- advice to heads, governors and teachers on the content of a policy statement for library and information service provision within the school. Support for the school by assisting in the development of methods by which the policy can be monitored.

5.11 *Professional support to Local Education Authorities*

- information and advice on the management of change within the Education Service as it affects the school library resource centre. (This may be curriculum change as in the case of the National Curriculum, or organizational change as with Local Management of Schools.) The information and advice may be to schools or the Local Education Authority or most probably to both.
- advice to the Local Education Authority on the monitoring and evaluation of school library resource centres. (This will particularly relate to the various curriculum changes.)
- assistance in establishing a school library resource centre policy for the Local Education Authority. This statement should cover such key issues as policy, organization, management, staffing, resourcing, accommodation and support services. It would give guidance to schools on the level of library resource centre provision regarded by the Authority as appropriate. The policy document should serve not only as a focus for change but also as the terms of reference for evaluating school library resource centre and learning resource provision in schools.
- a key role as a training agent within the Authority. The Schools Library Service will be an initiator of training in fundamental areas of learning resource provision and use, e.g. the library resource centre in the curriculum; learning skills; materials selection; the organization and management of resources. Furthermore, the Schools Library Service will cooperate with and coordinate other training resources in the Authority, e.g. the advisory/inspection service; training officers in other departments of the Local Authority. The training brief for the Schools Library Service is a broad one. It will encompass chartered librarians, teachers, advisors/ inspectors, officers, governors, parents and pupils. However, LMS is leading to the delegation of training budgets to schools, and this factor needs to be taken into account when assessing how Schools Library Services should respond to training needs.
- a liaison link with the public library service. The public library service is an important part of the network of education

support. The curriculum is resourced to a great extent by the provision made to individual pupils, and their parents, by the public library. For example, local studies source material is a significant resource which can only be obtained from the public library. The Schools Library Service is a communicator and a facilitator between schools and the public service in ensuring that pupils obtain the resources and assistance required. The Schools Library Service can also assist in coordinating and/or targeting public library services to schools, e.g. for class visits; author visits; holiday activities.

● liaison with other local authority services, such as Museums, Arts, Archives – for provision to schools.

Service delivery

5.12 The pattern of management in Schools Library Services is at present undergoing change, following the implementation of the Education Reform Act and the impact of other cultural changes in local authorities. The major concern has been survival, because of budgetary constraints following LMS. As noted above at paragraph 5.3, the placing of Schools Library Services within local authorities has varied across the UK, and this variety of provision is likely to continue; as are the range of responses to change because of the differing starting points of Schools Library Services.[2]

5.13 In an environment where a large proportion of schools manage their own budget, services – whether supplied centrally by the education authority or bought in – will be subject to close and critical scrutiny. Just as other local authority services have had to become more responsive to their clients, so the Schools Library Service will have to meet the changing needs of schools. They are the clients of Schools Library Services. Local authorities continuing to supply a centrally funded Schools Library Service will be providing one of the few major direct services to all schools. Consequently, clear aims and objectives will need to be set for the Schools Library Service and it will need to be carefully monitored and evaluated.

5.14 It is evident that, irrespective of the favoured model of service delivery in an education authority, appropriate staffing and funding are prime issues.

Staffing

5.15 The staffing structure of the Schools Library Service will derive from the model of service delivery adopted. However, in all structures the post of Principal Librarian or Senior Library Advisor, which heads the service, will be a key one.

5.16 The post of Principal Librarian or Senior Library Adviser is a prime focus for the maintenance of service standards and the development of school library resource centres and education within an authority. Some of the key responsibilities of the post are as follows:

Professional support

- To advise the Authority on the need for support services and to recommend service developments.
- To advise heads and governors on the design, organization, management, development and review of school library resource centres.
- To advise governors and head teachers on the appointment of Head of Library and Information Services and other staff for the school library resource centre.

Monitoring

- To monitor standards of service and of learning resources provision in schools and to recommend measures to ensure their continuing development.
- To participate in school inspections, advising on standards of learning resources provision and on the effectiveness of school library resource centre support for the curriculum.

Evaluation

- To appraise the work of the Head of Library and Information Services and advise head teachers on present performance in the post.
- To evaluate the performance of learning resources in all phases of education, against the Local Education Authority's school library resource centre policy.

Management

- To manage the budget, staff and all other areas connected with the delivery of the Schools Library Service.

To carry out these functions, the Principal Librarian or Senior Library Advisor should have responsibilities within departments responsible for libraries and for education and have clear lines of communication and authority within both departments.

5.17 The levels and nature of support staffing, both professional and clerical, involved in operating the Schools Library Service will properly derive from the model of service delivery favoured by an Authority.

5.18 In situations where the public library service acts as an agent for the Education Department there are obvious benefits to be derived from the coordination of school and public library services. However, there are also potential disadvantages, and it must be remembered that in those authorities where Schools Library Service and public library service posts are shared functions that the time available for work in schools must be adequate to meet demands.

Schools Library Services and the Local Education Authority
5.19 Local Education Authorities will be concerned to support pupils' learning opportunities in the most economic and effective way possible.

5.20 New styles of learning and the impetus provided by curriculum development, particularly the National Curriculum, have created unprecedented demands for resources of all types in schools.

5.21 The ability of the Schools Library Service to purchase in multiples, to exchange library collections and provide short term project loans, makes for an efficient and cost effective operation.

5.22 Materials no longer useful in one school can be redeployed efficiently in another.

5.23 Such centrally organized stock control can lead directly to the identification of any shortfall within a school's own library resource centre collection. This results in the Schools Library Service advising the school on the management and development of its resources to the advantage of both pupils and staff.

5.24 In terms of the effective use of the chartered librarian's time in a school, the Schools Library Service can fulfil an important function as a centralized purchasing agent. The provision of already classified and catalogued materials, which are ready for the shelves on delivery to schools, liberates chartered librarians from time-consuming routines and enables them to concentrate on their prime task of supporting the learning process.

5.25 Monitoring and evaluation are key aspects of the Education Reform Act, and the Schools Library Service must be involved in that process. The inspection of schools and the monitoring of the curriculum cannot take place without considering resource-based learning and the contribution of the school library resource centre. The National Curriculum requires evidence of library skills and competence in using a wide range of resources by pupils. The skills, knowledge and experience of Schools Library Service staff will be a significant factor in the provision of an effective education service.

5.26 As the Local Education Authority becomes distanced from the daily administration of schools and the delivery of the curriculum, the role of the local authority inspectorate grows. It is important therefore that resource-based learning, in whatever shape and by whatever name, is an inherent part of the curriculum review process. Equally, school library resource centres, as the principal providers of learning support in schools, should be automatically included in programmes of inspection.

5.27 Some Local Education Authorities will still retain direct management responsibility for a proportion of their small primary schools. By their nature, such schools are often disadvantaged both by lack of pupil peer challenge within the curriculum and shortage of resources. Local Education Authorities should endeavour to ensure that such schools under their direct management have library resource areas which are properly equipped, furnished and funded. Furthermore, it is unlikely that these schools will be able to deliver the National Curriculum without the support of the Schools Library Service.

5.28 The Local Management of Schools provision of the Education Reform Act may affect both the nature and style of delivery of the Schools Library Service. However, the needs of schools for support in providing library and information services, and the consequent demands for in-service training, will remain as constant factors. Indeed, given the requirements of the National Curriculum and other curriculum innovations, those demands are likely to increase. Therefore, it is important that local authorities should give a high priority to sustaining all aspects of the Schools Library Service, particularly in the following areas:

- loans of materials – long term and short term;
- advice on policy formulation, library resource centre management, planning and refurbishment, staffing, development programmes;
- support through central purchasing schemes, exhibition collections, book-lists and bibliographical aids, in-service training;
- promotion of materials, library resource centre use and effective learning strategies – through book talks, book weeks, publicity, network development, information skills programmes.

Conclusion
5.29 The Schools Library Service has a broader and more important role to play than purely that of a materials provider. The proper organization, management, and use of resources within schools is essential if effective learning is to take place. Through its advisory work, the training it organizes, and the bibliographical and other support it provides, the Schools Library Service will significantly enhance the learning process in schools. Local Education Authorities who are concerned to maintain and develop library and information services in schools will wish to support and sustain the quality of service provided by the Schools Library Service. The role played by the Schools Library Service

as the principal resourcing agent of the learning process should not be underestimated at this time of great educational change.

Recommendations

5.30 **The Library Association recommends that**:

(a) a centrally provided Schools Library Service be offered by Local Education Authorities for the essential support of schools in their provision of effective school library resource centres.

(b) the role of such a Schools Library Service be wide-ranging, and include loans of materials, advice, support and promotion. In-service training will be of considerable importance.

(c) the management and delivery of Schools Library Services be related to local circumstances. There will be varying patterns, depending on such factors as relationships between Education and Library services in the Authority and the impact of the Education Reform Act.

(d) the post of Principal Librarian or Senior Library Advisor be seen as a key one in the development of school library resource centres within an Authority.

(e) adequate funding be made available to provide for the staffing and resourcing of a Schools Library Service, recognizing that Schools Library Services are the most economical means of providing a wide range of support materials and professional advice for schools.

References

1 Committee of Inquiry into the Education of Children from Ethnic Minority Groups, *Education for all*, HMSO, 1985. (The Swann Report).

2 Heeks, P., *School library services today*, British Library, 1990, (British Library Research and Development Report 6024).

Further reading

Department of Education and Science, *A survey of secondary schools in six local education authorities: a report by Her Majesty's Inspectors*, DES, 1985.

Edmonds, D. and Miller, J., *Public library services for children and young people: a statistical survey*, British Library, 1990 (Library and Information Research Report 72).

Heeks, P., *School libraries on the move: managing change in English local authorities*, British Library, 1988 (Library and Information Research Report 69).

Library and Information Services Committee (Scotland), *Library services and resources for schools education in Scotland*, Edinburgh, National Library of Scotland, 1985.

Parker, A., 'New skills, new opportunities: the role of in-service training', *International review of children's literature and librarianship*, **1** (1), 1986, 1–21.

Pearson, S., *A survey of public library services to schools and children in England and Wales, 1989–90*, Loughborough, Loughborough University Library and Information Statistics Unit, 1991.

Scottish Library Association, *The school library resource service and the curriculum 'before 5' to 'sixteen plus'*, The Scottish Library Association, 1985.

Wilkes, B., 'The School Library Service within the Advisory Service', *School librarian*, **39** (2), 1991, 48–50.

CONCLUSION

The guidelines and recommendations for the provision of learning resources in schools contained in this report have been based on the considerable first-hand experience of the contributors in the delivery of library and information services to children and young people in schools. Careful attention has also been paid to the findings of the now extensive range of research and developmental work undertaken by various bodies, including the Department of Education and Science, the British Library and The Library Association.

In The Library Association's previous guidelines for school library resource centres, *Library resource provision in schools* (1977), concern was expressed at the relatively poor provision for learning resources within school library resource centres, and the need for a reappraisal of priorities to satisfy the 'growing needs for library services in schools'. The situation has changed considerably since then. There is a welcome recognition on the part of many decision makers that the provision of learning resources through a well-equipped and staffed school library resource centre is essential for the effective delivery of the curriculum. The National Curriculum has placed huge new demands on learning resources. Despite this, there are still concerns about the lack of adequate provision in many schools. The most recent Report on the subject by Her Majesty's Inspectorate: *Library provision and use in 42 primary schools* (1991), emphasized once again the need for greater attention to this aspect of children's educational provision:

> Just over a quarter of the schools have unsatisfactory accommodation for library books and materials. Over a third are hampered by old, inappropriate or damaged book stock. Well over half have been unable to make satisfactory arrangements for staffing their libraries, resulting in inadequacies of library organisation. Furthermore, even with the help of additional

funding from parents and other sources, library funding is unmatched to current book costs and replacement needs. Monitoring and evaluation of library provision and use are weak in all but a handful of schools. The major handicap, found almost universally, centres on lack of a library policy.[1]

In these guidelines we have identified the functions of school library resource centres and of schools library services in delivering effective library and information services in schools. We have provided recommendations, to assist schools and local education authorities in developing policies for their management of these learning resources. Funding is a key issue. With the advent of Local Management of Schools the responsibility for allocating sufficient finance is being devolved increasingly to head teachers and governors. However, local education authorities also have a responsibility to ensure learning resources are sufficiently funded and well managed through their advisory services and through providing a Schools Library Service. Funding must be made available to safeguard and develop the provision of learning resources in schools at both local authority and school levels. Policy making needs to be complemented by adequate resourcing. We strongly recommend therefore that there is a recognition of the need in every school for effective school library resource centre provision, and that these funding considerations be taken into account at each relevant point in the guidelines and recommendations.

References

1 Department of Education and Science, *Library provision and use in 42 primary schools*, DES, 1991.

SCHOOL LIBRARIES AND THE CURRICULUM: A READING LIST

This short reading list compiled by Peggy Heeks is intended as an introduction to core publications, not as a comprehensive bibliography. The works listed show the current state of school libraries, perceptions of library effectiveness, and the relationship between information skills and school libraries. The final section covers Schools Library Services.

1 The current state of school libraries

Association of Chief Librarians (Northern Ireland), *Post-primary school and college libraries in Northern Ireland: a survey 1988*, Omagh, Western Education and Library Board, 1988.

A report based on questionnaire returns, interviews etc., which aims to show the current state of post-primary and college libraries, teachers' perceptions of their relevance, and comparison with published guidelines.

Association of Chief Librarians (Northern Ireland), *Primary school survey*, Armagh, Southern Education and Library Board, 1991.

This report derives from a questionnaire sent to a sample of 50 primary schools in each Board area, which achieved an 83% response. It covers both the quantity and quality of books, library organization and staffing, book use and comments on the Schools Library Service.

Department of Education and Science, *Library provision and use in 42 primary schools*, DES, 1991.

A report by HMI on visits carried out between September 1989 and July 1990 to schools in 20 local education authorities. Apart from the expected sections on accommodation, stock, finance etc., the report also marks the effect of the National Curriculum on library provision and use. An interesting appendix gives an age profile of the stock in seven central libraries.

Department of Education and Science, *Secondary school library survey*, DES, 1981.
In need of updating, but the only general survey of England. It has been widely used as the basis for local surveys.

Department of Education and Science, *A survey of secondary school libraries in six local Education Authorities*, DES, 1985 and 1990.
These are two reports by Her Majesty's Inspectors, the first on visits to 62 schools, the second on visits to 58 schools in a different group of authorities. The surveys are particularly valuable in showing the development over the period. However, both make clear that many secondary school libraries give cause for concern.

Heeks, Peggy, *School libraries on the move*, The British Library, 1988 (Library and Information Research Report 69). ISBN 0 7123 3166 2.
A review of secondary school library development in 83 English local authorities, with case studies of nine of these. The emphasis is on the conditions and strategies which advance change.

Library and Information Services Committee (Scotland), *Library services and resources for schools education in Scotland*, Edinburgh, National Library of Scotland, 1985. ISBN 0 94870 500 0.
The report of a working party on current provision, which covered primary, secondary and special schools, and the School Resource Centres which support their libraries. It ends with a section on key issues and recommendations.

Library and Information Services Council (Wales), *Libraries in maintained secondary schools in Wales*, Cardiff, LISC (Wales), 1990.
In 1987 LISC (Wales) carried out a questionnaire survey of secondary school library provision, which achieved a 60% response. This report is from a working party established by LISC (Wales) to study and interpret the statistics collected. Arrangement is under conventional headings – accommodation, stock etc. – but included also are sections on information technology in school libraries and information skills. Under each section the working party offers recommendations, usually in the form of standards of provision. The overall conclusion is that the picture, in general 'is extremely unsatisfactory'. Interestingly it looks to schools, rather than local authorities

or the DES, to develop policies to put the recommendations into practice, hoping 'that LMS will provide greater financial flexibility for schools to develop such a strategy'.

Pain, Helen, *School librarianship in the United Kingdom*, British Library, 1987 (British Library Information Guide 4). ISBN 0 7123 3089 5.

Useful summary of the state of school libraries in the United Kingdom, and of the role of professional librarians in schools, supplemented by 26 appendices, some giving previously unpublished information.

2 Developing effective libraries

Bradford Education Library Service, *The effective junior and middle school library*, City of Bradford Metropolitan Council, 1990. ISBN 0 948989 05 X.

A guide to library planning, policy, management and monitoring, which forms part of the authority's *Framework for development* series, designed to assist implementation of the National Curriculum. A guide to libraries in Upper Schools, *Learning centres: the school libraries of the future*, was published in 1985 and was due for revision in 1991/92.

Department of Education and Science, *Better libraries: good practice in schools*, DES, 1989. ISBN 0 85522 210 7.

An attractive booklet describing 'some of the most encouraging practice seen by HM Inspectorate library specialists' in English primary and secondary schools in the period 1986–9.

Devon Education/Devon Libraries, *Resources for learning*, Exeter, Devon County Council, 1990. ISBN 1 85522 051 2.

A handbook prepared as part of Devon's school inspection and review programme, to ensure consistent guidelines, but also intended to help teachers appraise their library's ability to resource the curriculum effectively. It is proposed that the assessment is carried out through analysis of statistical data, observation and discussion, and that it should address both the role of the library and the level of provision. This guide is clearly presented, practical in approach and is likely to have a use far beyond Devon.

Education Publishers Council, *The book check action file: guidelines for governors and teachers in primary schools*, Publishers Association, 1989. ISBN 0 85386 174 9. Also *The book check action file: guidelines for governors and teachers in secondary schools*, Publishers Association, 1989. ISBN 0 85380 167 6.

These two volumes offer guidelines for governors and teachers on assessing school book needs.

Essex Education and Library Service, *Book policy in the primary school*, Longman, 1988. ISBN 0 582 02817 5.

A clear guide compiled by Essex teachers, librarians and language support staff, and designed as a basis for discussion and decision within schools. It includes many suggestions for promoting book use, and also pays attention to provision for children with special needs.

Heeks, Peggy, *Assessing school libraries*, The British Library, 1988 (British Library Research Paper 42). ISBN 0 71233 167 0.

Case studies of six Berkshire secondary schools designed both to document good practice and to demonstrate a methodology for assessment.

Herring, James, *School librarianship*, 2nd edition, Clive Bingley, 1988. ISBN 0 85157 423 8.

A revised edition of a standard work which offers guidance on library management and selection, organization and exploitation of resources.

McDonald, Margaret Marshall (ed.), *Towards excellence: case studies of good school libraries*, The Library Association, 1985. ISBN 0 85365 856 0.

A description of 10 United Kingdom schools, which shows libraries playing a full part in school life and suggests the reasons for such success.

Pain, Helen and Lesquereux, John, *Studies in school library management, I and II*, The School Libraries Group of The Library Association, 1985 and 1986.

Key questions and exercises designed to help school library development. Volume I is concerned with developing library policy, Volume II with the school librarian's role in implementing that policy.

School libraries: the foundations of the curriculum, Report of the
Library and Information Services Council's Working Party on
School Library Services/Office of Arts and Libraries, London,
HMSO, December 1984 (Library Information Series 13). ISBN 0
11630 713 7.

The report of a working party established by the Library and
Information Services Council for England, which is probably
the most influential report on school libraries of the past decade.
It puts forward three theses: that school libraries play a central
role in educating children to use information; that school
libraries are under-used; that they are also under-funded. The
report ends with a series of specific recommendations.

School Library Association, *Steps in the right direction*, Swindon,
SLA, 1989. ISBN 0 90064 151 7.

Practical guidelines for establishing, operating and promoting
the school library resource centre.

Scottish Library Association, *The school library resource service and
the curriculum 'before five' to 'sixteen plus'*, The Scottish Library
Association, 1985. ISBN 0 90064 957 7.

The report of a working party, which considers the educational
role of the library and offers guidelines on establishing effective
school libraries.

Wiltshire County Council, *Making libraries work*, Wiltshire County
Council, 1989. ISBN 0 86080 191 8.

Guidelines for relating school libraries to the curriculum,
designed to provide a measure against which the effectiveness
of schools' library resources can be assessed.

3   Information skills and curriculum initiatives

Gawith, Gwen, *Library alive!*, Black, 1987. ISBN 0 71362 900 2.

Full of practical suggestions for promoting reading and research
in the school library; especially suitable for the 9–13 age group.
Companion volumes are *Information alive!* Longman Paul, 1987
and *Reading alive!* Black, 1990.

Griffiths, Vivien (ed.), *The resource implications of GCSE*, Youth
Libraries Group of The Library Association, 1989. ISBN 0 94658
110 X.

A publication produced in collaboration with the School Libraries Group, consisting of a sequence of essays showing the impact of GCSE for both school and public libraries.

Howard, Julie, *Information skills and the secondary curriculum*, The British Library, 1991 (Library and Information Research Report 84). ISBN 0 71233 255 3.
A study of information skills teaching in GCSE programmes, and the role of school libraries in this work, with material drawn from a survey of LEAs in England and Wales, as well as case studies. The final chapter lists factors associated with successful implementation of skills programmes, and presents recommendations for improving practice.

Kinnell, Margaret and Pain-Lewins, Helen (eds.), *School libraries and curriculum initiatives*, Taylor-Graham, 1988 (British Library Research & Development Report 5969). ISBN 0 94756 838 7.
The report of two symposia for senior practitioners and policy makers which considered how the school library's role in developing and implementing new curriculum initiatives might be fulfilled. The recommendations call for greater commitment to this curriculum support role at both national and local level.

Lesquereux, John and Pain, Helen, *Studies in school library management III*, The School Libraries Group of The Library Association, 1987. ISBN 0 94893 309 7.
This third pamphlet in a series takes as its focus the library and the curriculum. Through key questions and discussion activities, librarians are brought to a clearer understanding of the curriculum and the school librarian's role in curriculum planning.

Lincoln, Paul, *The learning school*, The British Library, (Library and Information Research Report 62), 1987. ISBN 0 71233 135 2.
A case study of one school's attempt to develop resource-based learning, and the support needed from the library in that process.

Markless, Sharon and Lincoln, Paul (eds.), *Tools for learning: information skills and learning to learn in secondary schools*, British Library, 1986. ISBN 0 71233 085 2.
A stimulating training package for teachers and librarians on

promoting information skills in secondary schools. Edited by Sharon Markless and Paul Lincoln from materials produced by Terence Brake as director of the Information Skills in the Curriculum Research Unit.

Marland, Michael (ed.), *Information skills in the secondary curriculum*, Methuen Educational, 1981. ISBN 0 42350 910 1.
A seminal book, setting out the need for information-handling skills, and suggesting ways in which schools can develop these across the curriculum – a process in which libraries have a key role.

National Council for Educational Technology, *Information pack for school librarians*, Coventry, NCET, 1990.
A pack of photocopiable sheets which aim to raise awareness of the role of the school library in the curriculum, and the opportunities offered by information technology to enhance that role. The pack will help support claims for well resourced libraries, but in addition it contains information on contacts, materials and NCET projects of considerable practical value to school library staff. This is only one of a number of packs produced by NCET which relate to school libraries. Other 1990 titles include *Supported self study information pack* and *Developing partnerships between librarians and teachers in flexible learning*.

4   Schools Library Services

Heeks, Peggy, *School Library Services today*, British Library, 1990 (British Library Research and Development Report 6024).
Deals particularly with the effects of the Education Reform Act on Schools Library Services and trends in service development. This is the initial report of a research project based at Loughborough University: the final report is expected to be published in 1992.

Pearson, Stephen, *A survey of public library services to schools and children in England and Wales, 1989 – 90*, Loughborough University, Library and Information Statistics Unit, 1991. ISBN 0 94884 836 7.
The most comprehensive statistical survey available of Schools Library Services, covering budgets, stock and staffing. There are plans for a new edition to be produced each year.

MEMBERS OF THE LIBRARY ASSOCIATION'S WORKING PARTY ON LEARNING RESOURCES IN SCHOOLS

Wendy Drewett (Chair), Senior Assistant County Librarian (Schools and Children), Buckinghamshire County Library

Nigel Akers, Head of Library and Information Services, Djanogly Community Library, Djanogly City Technology College, Nottingham

Virginia Berkeley (until April 1989), Principal Learning Resources Adviser (Libraries), ILEA.

Rosemary Clements, Formerly Assistant County Librarian, Youth Services, Western Education and Library Board, Northern Ireland.

Ellen Dickie, Principal School Librarian, Central Regional Council School Library Service, Stirling

Ann Hobart, Assistant Director of Service Provision, The Library Association

Gillian Johnson, Principal Librarian, Schools and Children's Services, Doncaster Library and Information Services

Helen Lewins (until February 1989), Lecturer, Department of Information and Library Studies, Loughborough University

Martin Molloy, Assistant Director of Education, Derbyshire County Council

Observers

Peter Beauchamp, Office of Arts and Libraries

Stewart Robertson, Her Majesty's Inspectorate

Editor

Margaret Kinnell, Senior Lecturer, Department of Information and Library Studies, Loughborough University

Peggy Heeks contributed the final section of Further Reading